NOV 19 '04

By the Same Author

Insect Behavior
Insects and How They Function
The Evolution of Insects
The Magnificent Birds of Prey

Bird Behavior

by Philip S. Callahan

FOUR WINDS PRESS   NEW YORK

LIBRARY OF CONGRESS CATALOGING IN PUBLICATION DATA

Callahan, Philip S.
  Bird behavior.

  Bibliography: p.
  Includes index.
  SUMMARY: Describes bird anatomy and discusses such
aspects of bird behavior as feeding, reproduction, nesting,
defenses, migration, and bird communication.
  1. Birds—Behavior—Juvenile literature.
[1. Birds—Habits and behavior] I. Title.
QL698.3.C34 598.2'5 74–30309
ISBN 0–590–07309–5

Published by Four Winds Press
A Division of Scholastic Magazines, Inc., New York, N.Y.
Copyright © 1975 by Philip Callahan
All Rights Reserved
Printed in the United States of America
Library of Congress Catalog Card Number: 74–30309
5 4 3 2 1
79 78 77 76 75

JH
598
c.1

Contents

1. Introduction: Birds around Us   13

2. Biological Architecture: The Form of Birds   20

3. The Call to Dinner   38

4. Reproduction: Survival Chain   52

5. Nests and Nesting   64

6. Of Home and the Weather: Where Birds Live   78

7. Bird Territories   96

8. Bird Defense: To Live Another Day   107

9. Bird Journeys: Migration and Dispersal   120

10. Bird Communication: Song and Display   135

11. Fun with Birds   151

    Glossary   173

    Selected Reading   180

    Index   183

In memory of my father, Col. Eugene C. Callahan, cheerful patron of my nature studies,
                              and for
my mother who always insisted that without an education there was no such thing as the "good life."

Acknowledgments

I offer a very special thanks to my two young photographic assistants, Kevin Callahan and George Person, for without their help many of the bird photographs in this book could not have been obtained. Thanks go also to Dr. William Hardy who reviewed the manuscript for content. The scanning electron microscope photographs were taken by Thelma Carlysle and the author and are used with permission of the United States Department of Agriculture.

Bird Behavior

Figure 1–1. Male red-winged blackbird giving a territorial song near its cattail marsh home.

1. Introduction: Birds around Us

MOST OF US AT ONE TIME OR ANOTHER LIKE TO REMINISCE. I cannot say for sure how, or why, I developed my interest in birds, except that they are fascinating creatures. As I think back, I can barely remember the first stirrings of my interest in birds.

When I was a boy growing up in Memphis, a large, wooded lot separated our house from some nearby railroad tracks. Close by were a small creek and cattail marsh with a huge— at least it seemed so then—trestle passing over them. My parents warned me to keep off the trestle, but I was intrigued by the birds with the bright red wing patches that flew in and out of the mysterious marsh. I climbed the trestle to get a better look at them. Then my father explained that they nested in the marsh and that it would be far safer if I just waded into the cattails, mud and all, to find them. He pointed out that I could see the young in the nest far better from ground level than from the high trestle. They were red-winged blackbirds (Fig. 1–2).

He also loaned me his army pup tent so I could sleep out in the wooded lot and find out what bird produced the clear, pleasing warble I heard through my open bedroom windows on those fresh May mornings. Finally I spotted a small, blue-headed, red and green bird. This was my first introduction to the beautiful painted bunting of our Southern woodlands (Fig. 1–3).

During my boyhood in the early thirties the city fathers did not seem to mind an odd woodlot or a little cattail marsh in the midst of their city. Later, however, in the forties and fifties, people seemed bent on paving over all the little islands of nature that survived. Few of these little ecological pockets were spared from the bulldozer, developer, or highway engineer. The ones that did escape survived because a few obstinate and independent landowners thought more of their trees and cattails than the conveniences of civilization.

Later my family moved to Denver, where I was introduced to the birds of the prairies and mountains. From my window overlooking a large spruce-lined parkway I could hear the clatter of noisy house sparrows mixed with the intermittent "oooh, cooo, cooo, cooo" of the mourning doves. My pocket *Red Book of Birds of America* stated that the best-known characteristic of the mourning dove is its drawn out call of hopeless sorrow. However, I was not taken in by this description. To an alert fourteen-year-old it represented the awakening of spring and not a call of sorrow. Everyone has a favorite sight or sound that alerts the senses and brings out a nostalgic recollection of youth. Even today, when I hear the quiet call, my mind goes back to the long rows of tall, blue spruce trees that lined the parkway and the doves in them. The trees were a delight to climb, for their limbs grew straight out from the trunks and began at ground level.

There were at least half a dozen of these graceful trees that

Figure 1–2.   Nest of the red-winged blackbird. The nest is a deep bowl of woven layers of sedge grass. It is sometimes found in small trees or bushes but more often supported by surrounding marsh grasses two or three feet above the ground.

contained the makeshift nests of doves. Almost every morning on the way to school, I would climb each of the trees to observe the progress of incubation. This, however, involved considerable danger to the domestic life of the doves. The mother would often sit tight as I climbed closer and closer, until at the last moment she would burst forth, and the loosely assembled nest would tremble and shake, causing the white eggs to roll about on the flat surface.

Besides my *Red Book of Birds of America* I also had *Blue* and *Green* books. Those were the days when a ten-cent store actually was a ten-cent store, and the pocket-sized red, green, and blue bird books, with their stilted color photos, sold for

ten cents each. They were narrow—barely three inches wide
—and were thin enough to slide easily into my trousers
pocket. From these little books I learned to identify many of
the birds I saw.

It was Arthur A. Allen's *Book of Bird Life*, printed in
1930, that first led me to look closely at the behavior of the
birds I had learned to identify in the field. I was excited by
his marvelous photographs (for those days) and poured over
his book for hours at a time. It was my first introduction to
what the word "ecology" really means. Dr. Allen related the
birds to their habitat and to other living things, and that is

Figure 1–3.   The beautiful male painted bunting of our southern
woodlands. The male painted bunting is the most colorful of all
American birds. The species is not often seen because of its quiet
manner and the fact that it spends most of its time in dense,
brushy woodlots or river bottoms.

what ecology is all about. It is the study of the relationship of living things to their environment.

Although we hear much about ecology these days, it is not a new science, and many people like Dr. Allen were pleading with the American public to take a broader view of our natural resources and of the wildlife in our vast and wonderful country. With his wise words he reached a far greater audience of Americans than any bird writer up to that time.

It seems that many of us, perhaps a greater majority than we know, are born with some innate love of nature. We do not know why it is so. We only know that the sight of an insect on a dew-covered flower or of a white ibis flying against the evening sky stirs our senses and our inner being to some unexplainable longing for, and pleasure in, nature. Birds seem to arouse such feelings more than any other living creatures. I am sure some psychologist could explain this infatuation with living things and perhaps even relate it to our own evolution from forest to city. We are not interested in such explanations, however, for we can enjoy the creatures that share our planet without any need to justify or explain our own behavior. We are bird lovers because we love birds, and that's that!

The vast number of people, old and young, that belong to the National Audubon Society is proof enough that a good percentage of our population has an innate love of birds. Bird books are the most numerous and most popular of all nature books. Almost every state has its own state bird book. Some of the best are listed here in Selected Reading. Most of the bird books are written with the identification of birds in mind and usually contain some information on the life histories of the birds. There are also many excellent books on special groups of birds—shore birds, game birds, owls, and so forth.

I think that Dr. Allen's book was unique, however, because it used different species of birds to give the ecological or whole view of bird life. He showed his young readers how different species of birds fit into different ecological niches. We define "niche" as all of the physical and biological factors that control the life of an organism. For instance, physical factors could include soil, water, climate, and so forth, and biological factors, such things as food, availability of mates, type of plant life for cover and nesting. A habitat is a niche because it supplies all the factors which are necessary for the successful existence of an organism.

The niche of the red-winged blackbird that I studied as a boy is the cattail marsh and the land around it where the birds fly to feed. It builds its nest in the protective shelter of the impenetrable marsh, but it flies out to the fields to feed on weed seeds and insects. The marsh is its reproductive niche; the field of weeds and insects is its feeding niche. Both areas form the habitat of the black-coated, cheerful redwing. His persistent, happy "o-ka-lee" from the top of a swaying cattail proclaims to all the world that the marsh is his home. He is a feathered optimist, and he pours forth his optimism for all to hear.

If we look up in the sky and see a formation of Canada geese flying south in their typical V formation, we are thrilled by the sight. The feeling is much more meaningful, however, if we know why geese, and also other species, fly in a V formation. A knowledge of the science of birds (called ornithology), of the why and how of what birds do, does not diminish our joy in them one bit. In fact, it gives us a deeper appreciation of those beautiful creatures. If we have a true desire to know birds, we should not limit ourselves to identification alone. That is not what is meant by "bird watching," although some people seem to think so.

We know much more about the habits and behavior of birds now than we did when Arthur A. Allen wrote his book. Scientific knowledge in every field has increased a thousand-fold since the early thirties. We even know why geese fly in a V formation (see Chapter 8). It is not the purpose of this book to teach you to identify birds, but rather to give you a view of how birds fit into their environment and how they relate to people and other living creatures.

It is one of the sad facts of modern civilization that when we destroy a habitat, we destroy the birds that live in that habitat. If it is a small habitat in the city, such as the red-winged blackbird marsh, then the birds go elsewhere to nest and feed. If, however, we destroy the total habitat of a bird and if it is a specialized bird that fits into a special ecological niche, then we destroy a whole species—we cause the species to become extinct. Man loses one more thread of his being that makes him at one with nature. The ivory-billed woodpecker disappeared because people cut down, not a few, but every last virgin hardwood forest in the bottomlands of the South.

Some selfish people say, "So what? We needed the wood but not the woodpeckers." Because of this attitude the bottomland forests and woodpeckers disappeared. The people that try to justify such total destruction maintain that all living things evolve, reside for a time on earth, and then become extinct. From our study of evolution we know this to be true. However, our knowledge of evolution does not justify man's speeding the extinction of any living creature. Humans are not smart enough to decide what creature should or should not continue to exist. As we read on, we will see how complex the relationships are between all living things and the environment.

2. Biological Architecture: The Form of Birds

THE BEHAVIOR OF BIRDS DEPENDS ON THE SPECIAL SHAPE AND form of each individual species. Birds fit their environment: that is, they live, reproduce, feed, and move about—according to how efficiently their particular form enables them to function in their particular environment. Each species has evolved its form over many, many centuries, and the environment has helped to shape that form. This is true of all living things, plants as well as animals. Thus we would not expect a woodland bird, such as the painted bunting, suddenly overnight to adapt to a new life in the cattail marsh of the redwinged blackbird. Nor would we expect an owl that has evolved to hunt in the dark to change its habits to hunt during daylight.

Owls have developed eyes that are placed forward in their heads like the eyes of humans. Their eyes are very efficient light-gathering organs and are suited to flying at night when the overall light intensity is very low. Even a person who knows nothing about birds would place different species of owls together in one group because of their strange ways.

Figure 2–1.   Little blue penguin of New Zealand and Australia. This species, called the little penguin in Australia and the blue penguin in New Zealand, is both little—half the size of other species—and slate-blue on the back. Penguins catch their food underwater so their wings have evolved as powerful flippers. Their feet are webbed but are used only for steering. Propulsion is solely from the powerful flippers. The stout webbed feet are set far back on the body, giving the bird its upright walk. The special shape and form of the penguin fit it to a water environment.

It is not always simple to classify birds, however, and before we can understand why taxonomists (people who study classification) put certain birds together in one group, we must understand the generalized form of birds. It is the variations from that generalized form that fit each family and species of bird to its environment. Form determines not only where a bird lives, but also the behavior of each species. The diagram of the woodpecker illustrates the generalized form and the specialized terminology used to describe the external anatomical regions of the bird (Fig. 2–3).

Figure 2–2. Young Florida gallinule. Note the long slender toes, a modification well suited to the habitat of the gallinule. The wings of the young bird have clawlike appendages on the leading edge. The fingers of birds fuse to support the tip of the wing. In young gallinules, however, one finger remains separate and, along with the rest of the undeveloped wing, serves as a hand to aid the bird in climbing among the tangle of grass and floating water plants of its marshy habitat. As the wing develops the adult loses the claw, but the long toes are a great aid in running over floating leaves and lily pads.

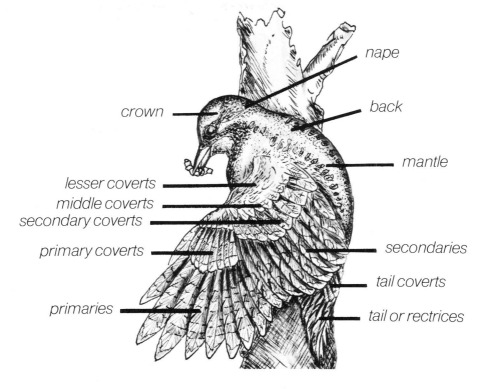

Figure 2–3. Female yellow-bellied sapsucker showing the generalized topographical regions of the body.

Figure 2–4. Great horned owl. This is a Texas great horned owl, which is lighter in color than its northern relative. Although owls hunt their prey mainly by sound, the eyes are efficient light-gathering organs under low light conditions. It is not true, however, that owls have difficulty seeing in the daylight. Under bright light conditions, the iris closes down so that the black pupil decreases in size to adjust to bright light.

THE FEATHERS

Birds, of course, are the only animals that possess feathers. Feathers, like hair on animals, grow from the skin. They are, however, a much more complex covering than simple hair. Feathers have no nerves in them, so if we cut a feather the bird feels no pain. Like fur, feathers insulate the body, but unlike fur, they perform a second function: without them birds could not fly. If we look at a feather with a scanning electron microscope we see that it has a very complex structure (Fig. 2–5 and 2–6).

Feathers grow from the body in lines called *tracts*. The open areas of skin between the feather tracts are called *apteria* and are sometimes covered with down. The feather tracts are shown in Figure 2–7 and are named for the parts of the birds they cover. Each feather tract is also subdivided into regions. Thus the *capital* tract that covers the top of the head is divided into a *frontal* region (near the beak), *coronal* region (top of head), and *occipital* region (back of head). The feathers along the feather tracts are for protection of the body and insulation (temperature control), not for flight.

The feathers of the wing and tail are designed for flight. The feathers of the tail vary in length with different species of birds, but generally they function as a rudder and as a brake in flight for all species.

Tail and wing feathers differ from the tract feathers in that they are attached to bones. The tail feathers are called the *rectrices* and attach to the last bone of the backbone, called the *pygostyle*. The pygostyle is modified by the fusion of several bones to hold the tail feathers.

The flight feathers of the wing attach to the bones of the wing. The outer wing feathers, called *primaries*, attach to the *digits* and to the fused *carpal-metacarpal* bones (carpometa-

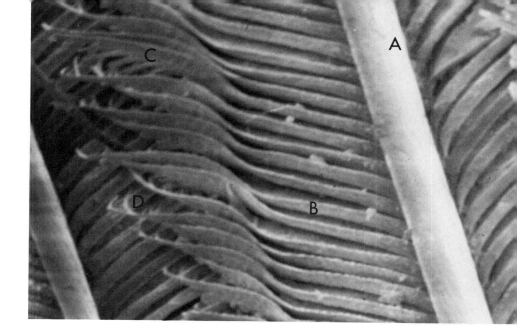

Figure 2–5. Scanning electron microscope photograph of the secondary feather of a red-tailed hawk (magnified 400 times). A. Barb; B. Barbules; C. Barbicels (like a fringe on the barbules); D. Hamuli.

Figure 2–6. Scanning electron microscope photograph of the barbicels and hamuli (magnified 1,000 times). A. Barbule; B. The barbicels are like a fringe on the larger barbules; C. The tips of the barbicels are curved to form the hamuli.

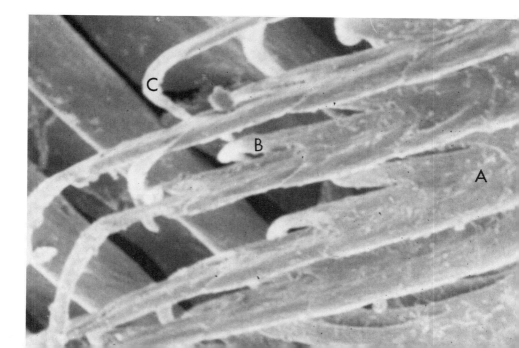

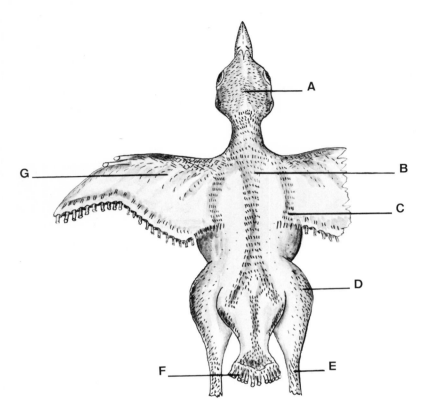

Figure 2–7. Feather tracts—dorsal view. A. *Capital* tract—head; B. *Spinal* tract—neck to rump; C. *Humeral* tract—shoulder region; D. *Femoral* tract—thigh; E. *Crural* tract—leg; F. *Caudal* tract—tail region, including the rectrices; G. *Alar* tract—all of the wing, including the primaries and secondaries. The *ventral* tract is all of the feathers on the underparts of the bird.

carpus) at the end of the wing. The *digit* and *carpal* bones of the birds are comparable to finger and wrist bones in humans.

The inner wing feathers are called *secondary* feathers and are attached to the *ulna,* one of the two bones (the ulna and *radius*) that make up the middle part of the wing. They both connect to the large *humerus,* the bone that attaches the wing to the bird's shoulder.

Birds that fly may have from nine to twelve primary feathers, although a flightless bird, the ostrich, has sixteen primaries. The number of secondaries may vary from six to thirty-two depending on the species.

A species' flying characteristics depend to a great extent on the shape of the wing and tail feathers. We will discuss that more fully in Chapter 9.

A feather is a marvelous piece of engineering. There are few structures in nature that are stronger, lighter, or more flexible than the feather.

The shaft of the feather is called the *rachis*. The base of the feather, called the *calamus,* is hollow, and the end is embedded in the feather follicle of the skin from which the feather grows. The *vanes* of the feather on either side of the

Figure 2–8.   Tail feathers (retrices) from eight different species of birds. Left to right: 1. Cardinal; 2. Yellow-shafted flicker (note how the tip is pointed and very stiff for bracing against the side of a tree trunk) ; 3. American kestrel (falcon) ; 4. Blue jay; 5. Red grouse (Ireland) ; 6. Scissor-tailed flycatcher; 7. Cooper's hawk; 8. Magpie.

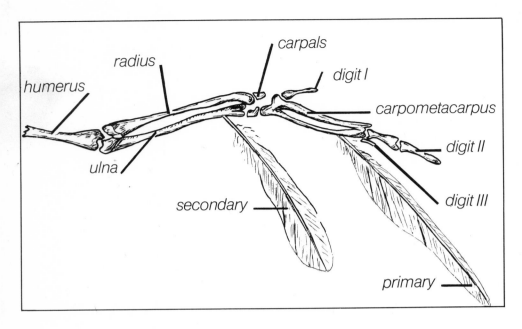

Figure 2–9. The wing bones of a bird. The primary feathers attach to the fused carpometacarpus. In man there are eight carpal (wrist) bones; in birds only two remain. The rest have fused with the three metacarpal (finger) bones to form the carpometacarpus. There are only three digits (finger tips) in the bird wing. The secondary feathers attach to the ulna.

rachis are made up of a series of branches called *barbs* (Fig. 2–5).

Barbs are like microscopic feathers, for they in turn are lined with minute filaments called *barbules*. The barbules are lined with a comb-like fringe made up of smaller filaments called *barbicels*. Some of the barbicels have a hooked tip called *hamuli* that serves to interlock the barbicels and hold them together in a tight flexible web. It is the hamuli of the barbicels that we will pull apart when we separate the veins of the feathers on either side of the shaft.

There are several different types of feathers. The feathers that form the outline of a bird are called *contour* feathers. The primaries, secondaries, and rectrices (tail) are the most developed of the contour feathers. *Semiplumes* are feathers that have a central shaft but are fluffy because they lack hooklets (hamuli) to hold the barbules together. *Bristles* around the mouth, eyes, and nostrils are modified feathers. *Filoplume* feathers are hair-like feathers that grow in groups (two to eight) around the base of the contour feathers. *Down* feathers are small soft feathers without veins. The shaft of the down feather is usually absent, and the barbs fan out from the tip of the calamus. Down feathers are concealed under the contour feathers in adult birds. The young of many birds are completely covered with down which is molted as the contour feathers replace them (Fig. 2–10).

Figure 2–10. Young black vulture. The young of many birds, especially birds of prey, are completely covered with down feathers which are molted as the regular contour feathers replace them. The naked head of the vulture is an adaptation that prevents the bird from dirtying its head while feeding on rotting carrion. Note the ear opening just behind the eye.

THE HEAD AND BEAK

The beak of a bird consists of the upper and lower *mandibles*. The space between the base of the beak and the eye is called the *lores,* and the region around the eye is the *orbital* region. Hawks and owls have a soft yellow covering at the base of the upper mandible called the *cere.* The *nose* or nostril is located on the cere in birds of prey and at the base of the beak in other birds. Special structures such as shields, combs, or wattles are found at the base of the upper mandible or on the head of certain birds. We are all familiar with the

Figure 2–11.   Beak of the American kestrel. The nostril is located on the soft membranous covering, called the cere, at the base of the beak. Hawks, owls, and parrots have ceres. Note the notched beak of falcons.

Figure 2–12. Tridactyl foot. The common Australian emu has only three toes. Members of the emu family are flightless. Emus depend on their legs for survival; they are swift of foot and rival the kangaroos in speed. Emus had become scarce in eastern Australia. They are now protected in the open forests and plains of the interior.

fleshy pad of skin called the *comb* on roosters. A *wattle* is a fleshy growth of skin that hangs from the chin, throat, or sides of the face. Roosters have a chin wattle. The opening of the ear is concealed beneath a patch of *auricular* feathers on the side of the head. The shape of the beak is dependent upon the food habits of the species (see Chapter 3).

THE LEGS AND FEET

The feet, like the beak, are modified according to the habits of the species. Usually the toes are arranged with three forward and one backward in what is called an *anisodactyl* foot. Some birds, such as owls, cuckoos, parrots, and woodpeckers, have two toes forward and two backward, a *zygodactyl* foot. Most American plovers and the auks and guillemots have

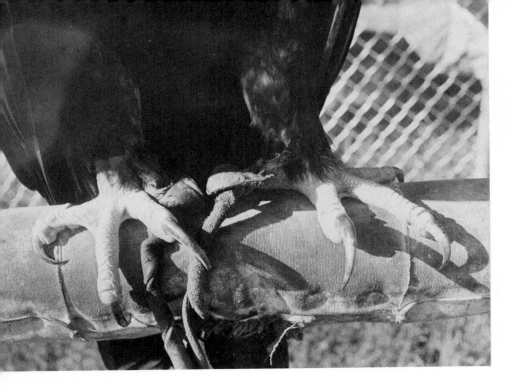

Figure 2–13. Anisodactyl foot. Most birds have three toes forward and one backward as this eagle. Feet are modified according to the habits of the bird. The strong claws of the eagle can close like a steel trap and the sharp talons pierce the vital organs of the prey.

tridactyl (three toes only) feet. There is also a three-toed woodpecker.

The thigh (femur bone) is hidden by the contour feathers of the body. For that reason the first visible joint in a bird's leg is not the thigh and knee joint but the feathered leg portion below the thigh called the *tibia* and ankle joint. The ankle joint of a bird is confused with the knee in other vertebrates (although it bends backward instead of forward as a true knee would) because of the long *tarsus* to which the toes attach. In humans the tarsal bones are a part of the foot, but in birds a tarsal bone, called the *tarsometatarsus*, is elongated and is part of the leg visible when a bird walks, hops, or perches (Fig. 2–14).

HOW BIRDS ARE CLASSIFIED

Although the classification of birds is based primarily on the morphology (form) of birds, nevertheless, from ancient times they have also been classified by habitat and also by habit. Thus Aristotle divided birds into land and water birds.

Frederick II of Hohenstaufen, Emperor of the Holy Roman Empire from 1212 to 1250, was also a brilliant medieval ornithologist. In his famous book, *De Arte Venandi Cum Avibus* (*The Art of Falconry*), he described the anatomy of birds in great detail. He was the first person to describe the hollow bones, structures of the heart and lung, and other organs. He also made significant contributions to the study of bird flight and migration. His book is considered a scientific work of the first order.

In Chapter 2 (Book I) he divides birds by habitat into waterfowl, land birds, and neutral birds. In Chapter 3 he divides birds by habitat into raptorial (hunting) and nonraptorial birds. If we read Frederick, we see that he means by neutral birds those that utilize both land and water. He writes:

> There are still other birds that remain as much in the water as on land, like the cranes, both large and small, also both kinds of storks, the white and the black, the latter are frequently seen wandering about, fishing in water and in swamps and other wet places, returning afterwards to dry land.

Taxonomy is the science of the classification of living things. Modern taxonomists study the morphology of birds and group them by form. Those that are considered as having evolved from a single ancestral species, because they have certain characteristics in common, are placed in a single *family*. The falcons, for instance, are called Falconidae: *idae*

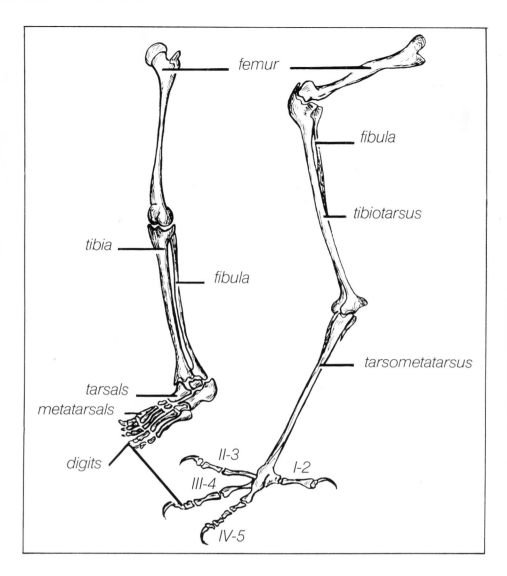

Figure 2–14. The leg bones of man and bird. The thigh of man (femur bone) is visible but in birds it is concealed beneath the skin and feathers. The top visible portion of a bird's leg is supported by the fused tibiotarsal bone. The tarsal bones of man support the ankle. The lower portion of the bird's leg is supported by the remaining tarsal bones which are fused with metatarsal bones to form the tarsometatarsus. Thus the long lower portion of the bird leg is really an elongated foot. The four digits (I to IV) form the toes (claws) and are composed of 2, 3, 4, and 5 bones respectively.

is the ending for all bird families and is placed at the end of the Latin family name.*

Families are also grouped together according to certain morphological characteristics into *orders*. There are considered by most ornithologists to be twenty North American bird orders. The Latin order name always ends in *formes*, thus the order of ducks is Anseriformes, from the Latin Anser, which means goose. Ducks, geese, swans, and mergansers all belong to the Anseriformes.

Birds are further classified into higher man-made categories. They are a part of the animal kingdom, distinguished from the plant kingdom, and are placed in the phylum chordata. Chordata are animals that have a backbone and a dorsal (backside) central nervous system (spinal cord). The class name for birds is *Aves*, from the Latin noun for bird. The order and family mentioned before are also considered higher man-made taxonomic categories.

The lower categories are the *genus* and *species*. The classification of birds is complicated by the fact that most organisms have changed or evolved over long periods of time. Sometimes it is very difficult on the basis of form alone for a taxonomist to name a species. Any one species may have closely related look-alikes that may or may not be separate species. One indication of whether two look-alike species are the same or are different species is whether or not they mate and reproduce together. If they do, they are usually considered to be the same species.

For example, if we wish to classify a magpie according to where it fits in this man-made scheme, it would be listed as follows:

---

*For a detailed discussion of the classification of a group of animals see *The Evolution of Insects* by the author.

Kingdom	Animal
Phylum	Chordata
Class	Aves (feathered chordata)
Order	Passeriformes (perching birds)
Family	Corvidae (crow family)
Genus	*Pica*
Species	*pica*

The genus and species name are put together for the Latin binomial name of the bird; thus, the magpie's scientific species name is *Pica pica*. The genus first name is always capitalized but not the species second name.

Bird orders and families are usually listed from those considered lowest on the evolutionary scale to those considered highest. A listing of the orders with the common families in English is a great aid to remembering how the different families of birds are related to one another. The following list for the twenty orders and the families in each order of North American birds is taken from the list given by Van Tyne and Berger (*Fundamentals of Ornithology*, 1959).

ORDER	FAMILY
Gaviiformes	Loons
Podicipediformes	Grebes
Procellariiformes	Albatrosses, Shearwaters, and Storm-petrels
Pelecaniformes	Pelicans, Boobies, Tropic birds, Cormorants, Frigate-birds, and Anhinga
Ciconiiformes	Herons, Storks, Ibises, and Flamingos
Anseriformes	Ducks, Geese, and Swans
Falconiformes	Vultures, Hawks, Falcons, and Eagles

Galliformes	Curassows, Grouse, Pheasants, and Turkeys
Gruiformes	Cranes, Limpkins, and Rails
Charadriiformes	Oystercatchers, Plovers, Sandpipers, Avocets, Phalaropes, Skuas, Gulls, Skimmers, and Auks
Columbiformes	Pigeons
Psittaciformes	Parrots
Cuculiformes	Cuckoos
Strigiformes	Barn Owls and Owls
Caprimulgiformes	Nightjars and Nighthawks
Apodiformes	Swifts and Hummingbirds
Trogoniformes	Trogons
Coraciiformes	Kingfishers
Piciformes	Woodpeckers
Passeriformes (Perching Birds)*	Tyrant-flycatchers, Larks, Swallows, Crows (Magpies and Jays), Titmouse, Nuthatches, Creepers, Dippers, Wrens, Mockingbirds (Threshers, Catbirds), Thrushes, Old-World Warblers, Pipits, Waxwings, Silky-flycatchers, Shrikes, Starlings, Vireos, Wood-warblers, Blackbirds (Orioles), Tanagers, Weaverbirds (House Sparrows), and Finches (Sparrows, Grosbeaks, Buntings).

*The Passeriformes are called perching birds because their slender, rather elongated legs and toes are well-suited for perching on branches. The order contains the greatest number of commonly observed birds. For a complete review of bird families and species the reader should study one of the better field books of bird identification such as Roger Tory Peterson's *A Field Guide to the Birds.*

3. The Call to Dinner

BIRDS SPEND A LOT OF TIME FORAGING FOR FOOD. DR. N. A. M. Verbeek, an ornithologist at Redpath Museum, McGill University, Montreal, found that the yellow-billed magpie spends up to 46 percent of its time feeding. The magpie eats mainly insects and must spend a great deal of time feeding. It requires considerable energy for a bird to survive. If we watch small birds for very long we get the impression that they are very nervous, for they move about quickly. Large birds, such as hawks and sea gulls, seem to take life easier.

Birds have a high rate of metabolism. Metabolism is the process of chemical changes within living cells by which energy is provided for life activities and repair of the body. A high metabolic rate means that food energy is used up quickly.

It is well-established that the metabolic rate of small vertebrates, birds and other animals, is inversely proportional to their size, and thus large birds produce less heat in proportion to their size than small birds. The body temperature of birds is much higher than that of other vertebrates: the normal temperature of an active bird is 106° F.

I have kept many of the larger birds of prey and trained them for falconry. My trained golden eagle requires only one meal a day for good health. I found that Sultan—as I named him—could fast for a week at 65° F. with no ill effects whatsoever. No doubt during times of heavy snowfall on the prairie, eagles survive even longer fasts in the wild. A small house wren, however, would die in less than two days without food.

There is a well-known story about a man named John Phillips told by Dr. Allen in the May–June 1926 issue of *Bird Lore Magazine*. Mr. Phillips found a family of house wrens whose parents were killed by a cat. By working full time collecting insects he kept them quiet until breakfast time, but before breakfast was over the fledglings were again clamoring for food. Their gaping mouths seemed like the entrances to bottomless pits. The entire family plus the maid and butler

Figure 3–1. Sultan, the author's trained golden eagle, goes to school. Large birds such as eagles can go for much longer periods without food than very small birds.

Figure 3–2. The beak of the hermit thrush is narrow and tapers to a fine point. It is well suited for probing for insects in the forest floor.

Figure 3–3. The meadowlark, like the hermit thrush, feeds almost exclusively on the ground. Since it also feeds primarily on ground-dwelling insects, its beak is shaped much like that of thrushes. About 30 percent of its food is grass and weed seed, however, so the beak is heavier and stronger than that of the thrush. The meadowlark is not really a lark but a member of the blackbird family.

could not keep the birds satisfied. Mr. Phillips sent two of the men from his factory to the woods with axes to split open logs for ant eggs and grubs. Despite the combined efforts of six persons the little birds died of starvation! As Dr. Allen pointed out, the good-hearted gentleman worked nobly but in vain. How many Americans each spring find fledgling birds and have the same disappointing experience?

Bird seed suppliers for pets estimate that a single pet bird eats nearly one hundred times its own weight in seed per year. That would equal a person eating forty-five pounds of food a day. One can buy all kinds of bird seed, so it is much easier to keep a small seed-eating bird alive than a small insectivorous bird. It is always best when one sees a young fledgling bird on the ground or in the bushes to leave it where it is. Most fledgling birds live on animal food, and even the young of seed-eating birds, such as sparrows, are reared in the nest on insect food. Chances are that the parents are nearby and will respond to the call of a hungry fledgling. Because of its high rate of metabolism, it has a much better chance of survival even if only one parent feeds it.

THE SHAPE OF THE BEAK

The bird beak has evolved in association with the high metabolic rate and the development of flight. The beak of each bird is adapted for its own particular food habits. A bird's light, horny beak fulfills many functions besides feeding. In each kind of bird it is always the minimum size required for feeding, but it also serves to pick up things, for protection in a fight, and for nest building. The beak requires a much lighter jaw skeleton and less bulky musculature than the jaw of other vertebrates.

A bird's gastric tract (stomach area) is divided into two

chambers, the *proventriculus,* or real stomach, and the *ventriculus,* or gizzard. The gizzard is a muscular stomach and partially fulfills the same grinding function that teeth do in mammals. Most seed-eating birds swallow sand, pebbles, or other kinds of grit. This material helps in grinding the food and probably also provides trace minerals such as calcium and phosphorus.

A bird's beak, as a food-gathering tool, is shaped to fit the job. There are so many different types that it would be impossible to list them here. They range all the way from the large *gular* pouch of the pelican located below the beak for storing fish, to the small, delicate, pointed beak of wood warblers, useful for catching small insects.

Birds of prey have hooked beaks for tearing apart small pieces of meat. Contrary to popular belief, falcons, hawks, and eagles never use their beaks for defense. A cornered bird of prey will strike with its talons but not its beak. The falcon has a notch at the tip of its beak. A peregrine falcon, one of the fastest flying birds, dives on its prey from high above and in the open. The kill is accomplished by the *stoop,* or steep dive, during which the falcon hits with its open claws. Since ancient times it was believed that falcons killed by hitting the prey with the claw doubled up like a fist. Recent high-speed movies, however, show that the claws open up at the instant of strike and the hind talon rips the back of the prey. If the stoop does not kill the bird, the falcon bears it to the ground and breaks the vertebrae of the neck with the notch in its beak. Birds of prey usually rest after a kill and pluck a bird before eating it.

A parrot also has a hooked beak. (The parrot family includes macaws, love birds, parakeets, lories, and cockatoos.) In one respect their beaks are quite different from those of all other birds—the top mandible is movable. There is a trans-

Figure 3–4. One of the strangest beaks in the bird kingdom belongs to the toucan. The ungainly beak appears too heavy to carry but is in reality an extremely light and strong structure. It is very thin and is supported on the interior by a fine network of bony fibers. These are keel-billed toucans from Costa Rica; they feed primarily on tropical fruits, which they crush with the beak.

verse hinge between the upper mandible and the skull. The parrot has extremely strong beak muscles and can gnaw through thick wood. Its short, powerful hooked beak is ideal for cracking seeds. It also lends itself to use as a climbing tool. The parrot hooks it over uneven surfaces and pulls itself up a tree or the side of a cage.

Like parrots, crows, jays, and magpies have stout, powerful beaks. They are much longer, however, and are not designed for cracking seeds. The magpie beak is a generalized all-purpose beak. It is sturdy and used for probing under debris on the ground or for hammering dead wood and digging in soil for grubs. It is also used as a hammer to deliver sharp, heavy blows to acorns or other seeds to get inside them.

Figure 3–5. Male American kestrel. Hawks and falcons have strong claws for holding and hooked beaks for tearing flesh. This little kestrel holds a white-lined sphinx moth almost half as big as itself. The kestrel lives mainly on mice and insects.

Like squirrels, magpies store acorns. The yellow-billed magpie spends up to 20 percent of its time carrying and storing acorns in November and December.

Herons have long, pointed bills for spearing fish, frogs, crawfish, salamanders, and other small water creatures. The heron is one bird that does use its beak for defense. A wounded or cornered heron or bittern (a close relative) will strike with its sharp beak for the eye. In the Middle Ages kings hunted herons with the peregrine falcon. More than one favorite hunting falcon fell victim to the long dagger-like beak of the heron.

The snipe has a unique bill for probing the soft mud of bogs and tundra. It plunges its long beak into the mud and pulls out wireworms, crane-fly larvae, cutworms, and other soft-bodied earth dwellers.

The woodpecker's beak, however, is long and sharp like a chisel. After the beak has chiseled an opening to expose the larvae, the tongue is inserted into the deep cavity and pulls the wood-boring larvae out. It is modified so that it can extend far beyond the bill and reach into cavities for the larvae. It is attached to a set of supporting bones called the *hyoid apparatus*. The hyoid elements attach to the base of the tongue and loop over the skull.

The red crossbill has a peculiar beak that is crossed at the tip. Crossbills feed on pine seeds. A crossed bill would seem to be a poor instrument for picking up seeds, but the crossbill

Figure 3–6. The Australian cockateel has a short, hooked bill. The upper mandible of members of the parrot family is hinged to the skull, a modification that gives great leverage to the powerful beak and aids in cracking open hard seed. The hooked beak is also used as an aid for climbing up uneven surfaces.

picks up the seed with its tongue and uses the bill as a pry for wrenching open pine cone scales to get at the seeds.

An interesting legend from the Middle East holds that the little bird became stained red and twisted its beak attempting to pry the nails from Christ's palms. Folklore notwithstanding, the crossed bill is certainly designed for a specific feeding niche—the cones of pine trees. We see from these few examples that birds have developed a great variety of beaks, each useful to a species as a food-gathering tool.

WHERE BIRDS FIND FOOD

Not many years ago little was known of where birds found food, or even what they ate. The black-billed magpie, for instance, was considered a pest and was killed by farmers and ranchers on sight. Recent studies have shown it to be a beneficial bird.

Magpies inhabit open grasslands and river lands. The black-billed magpie ranges from the base of the Rocky Mountains westward. Now we know that three-fifths of the food magpies eat is of animal origin. Magpies find their food almost wholly on the ground. Their diet includes soil invertebrates, as well as insects clinging to vegetation. During the early fall, up to 50 percent of the magpie's diet consists of grasshoppers. The magpie is really the farmer's and rancher's friend. The magpie prefers animal food, but often must feed on plant food as well. (Birds which feed on both plant and animal food are called "omniverous.") During the winter months, for instance, seed and grain may make up 40 percent of its food, and carrion along the roadway, another 13 percent.

Although the feeding habits of the magpie restrict it to open spaces, it has one other requirement—water. Magpie nests are

Figure 3–7. Nest of little green heron. The beak of the heron is long and pointed for spearing fish, frogs, and other small aquatic creatures.

often found along small prairie waterways and arroyos. The magpie not only drinks and bathes, but spends a considerable amount of time soaking its food in water, especially hard grain. This strange feeding behavior may be for softening the food, but sometimes it even soaks soft food like carrion.

Civilization has changed the feeding range of many species of birds. Ornithologists believe that there are more robins in America now than when the white man first arrived on the continent. The robin feeds mainly on earth worms. It finds its dinner in moist, grassy, open shaded areas and so fits right in suburbia, where there are plenty of shady lawns.

The black vulture and turkey vulture are most often conspicuous along the highway feeding on carrion killed by automobiles. It is doubtful if formerly there were as many dead bodies in the woods as there are left slaughtered on our highways.

Figure 3–8. Dowitchers feeding. Dowitchers, sometimes called robin snipes, are the only snipes found on open seashores. Like its close relative, the common Wilson's snipe, it has a long beak for probing soft mud. Along shores it feeds on water beetles and various marine worms.

Some birds are, of course, limited as to their feeding territory. Restricted and specialized feeding habits tend to limit the distribution of certain species. The Everglade kite is close to extinction because of its very narrow food habits. This beautiful black bird of prey, a relative of the hawk, lives in the Everglades. Most kites are distinguished by their long narrow wings and light, graceful flight; however, the Everglade kite has broad wings. People who live around the Everglades often call it the small snail hawk or hook-bill hawk.

The Everglade kite feeds on snails of the genus *Ampullaria,* which come out of the water in the cooler part of the day.

The kite hovers over the water and drops down to pick up a snail, which it then carries to a perch in its talons. It holds the snail in one long claw and sits motionless. As the snail begins slowly to extrude from the shell, the kite grabs the body and pulls the snail out with its blunt-edged, deeply hooked beak. It throws the shell aside. In the Everglades the kite's eating areas are marked by piles of empty snail shells under the perch. This is one more example of a very specialized beak for a very specialized eating job.

As the Everglades are drained and the *Ampullaria* snail population reduced, the Everglade kite becomes more and more rare. The kite is also found in restricted feeding areas in Eastern Mexico, Cuba, and Central and South America. We hope it will survive in its more southern range.

In Ireland I have observed another specialized feeding habit. I once found a great tit nesting in a broken drain pipe near a thatched-roofed Irish cottage. I noticed that many small insectivorous birds busied themselves about old cottage

Figure 3–9.   Yellow-billed magpies feeding on a garter snake. The yellow-billed magpie is one of the few American birds whose range is wholly within the state of California. It is a beneficial bird that feeds over 50 percent on insects.

Figure 3–10. Australian kookaburra is a member of the king-fisher family but does not fish. It lives in the open savannah wood-lands of Australia where it feeds mainly on lizards and insects.

thatches, pecking and searching for insects. The hedge spar-row, in particular, regularly searches the eaves of thatched cottages for insects. Only the great tit, however, had sense enough to pull out straws from the thatch, dragging the insect out with the straw. An industrious great tit with a large family to feed could make the corners of a good thatch look quite ragged by pulling straws. I don't know if the Irish farmers take exception or not to this busy mite of a bird with its black cap and bib. The fact that tits are forever hanging upside down, busily gleaning insects from the farmyard and thatch should influence the farmer, despite an odd messy spot in the thatch.

Pulling the straw out with the bug is interesting behavior for another reason, however. Years ago anthropologists thought that only humans use tools. Later they changed their minds when primates were observed using sticks for poking termites out of the earth—clearly making use of the stick as a "tool." Today there are more and more reports of birds engaged in what behaviorists call "tool-use," as the tit uses the straw thatch to pull the bugs out. One ornithologist reports seeing the New Caledonian crow using a small twig to probe into the end of a hollow branch. Presumably it was probing for insects. The use of a twig as an insect probe during food searching has also been reported in two species of Galapagos finches. Perhaps birds are smarter than we think.

Although we have only given a few examples related to feeding, it is obvious that a considerable amount of any bird's behavior is associated with food gathering. An observant bird watcher should be able to predict where a bird feeds and what it feeds on by the type of beak it has. However, he may be fooled. The laughing kookaburra of Australia, also called the laughing jackass because of its loud laugh, is a kingfisher in the family Alcedinidae. The family is worldwide in distribution and includes the American belted kingfisher. The kingfisher is usually seen perched in trees along river banks or lake shores. Its beak is long, much deeper than wide at the base, and very powerful: it is ideal for catching fish. The kingfisher dives for its prey in the water, then flies to a perch where it pounds the fish to death and swallows it head first. The kookaburra is never found near water, but it uses the exact same technique to dispatch lizards, its favorite food. In Australia I have most often seen the kookaburra in savannah woodlands perched on huge whitened piles of dead gum tree limbs. There it waits patiently for an uncautious lizard to appear from underneath the tangled pile of wood.

The kookaburra has evolved feeding habits completely different from its fishing relatives. Its call to dinner is also unique. The bill is pointed skyward, and there issues forth a never-to-be-forgotten rollicking "koo-hoo-hoo-hoo-hoo-hoo-ha-ha-ha-ha-ha."

4. Reproduction: Survival Chain

A BASIC FACT OF LIFE IS THAT JUST AS FEEDING ASSURES THE survival of the individual, reproduction assures the survival of the species.

During the winter months birds are faced with the rigors of survival in cold weather or in a new territory if the species migrates. As the days get longer and the season progresses toward spring, important physiological changes occur in birds of both sexes. The changes are triggered by the climatic rhythm of the seasons. Ecologists call these changes that occur in the life cycle of living things throughout the seasons *phenological* events. The word "phenological" comes from the Latin for the word "phenomenon."

Phenology is the branch of science that deals with the relationship between climate and periodic biological phenomena, such as the flowering of plants, the fruiting of trees, the migration of birds, and so forth.

A bird's physiological reproductive changes are internal, but at the same time noticeable external behavioral traits indicate the approach of the nesting season. Specialized and complex bird ceremonies, termed by behaviorists "display," lead to courtship and *pair formation* between individuals of the species.

Most birds are monogamous, that is, during any one nesting cycle mating takes place only between a single pair. Since the pair normally remains together throughout the nesting period and usually for a period thereafter, behaviorists say a *pair-bond* is formed between the male and the female.

In the common type of pair-bond the sexes remain together until the young have been raised. Most migratory passerine birds seem to form this type of pair-bond. Everyone is familiar with the clamoring robin or mockingbird that has left the nest and is seen begging for insects from both its attentive parents. The parent birds have remained together to feed the young.

Some species are believed to form life-long pair-bonds. Swans, eagles, geese, ravens, and even little white-breasted nuthatches may form such enduring bonds. Most ducks form a pair-bond months before the nesting season but do not necessarily remain together all year long. A few species of birds, such as the male and female grouse, meet only to copulate. Since more than one male may copulate with a single female, such a behavior does not represent a true pair-bond.

BIRD DISPLAY

By the word "display," behaviorists generally mean movements, postures, or sounds of a specialized type, which have the capacity to initiate specific responses in another individual, usually of the same species. The famous animal behaviorist Konrad Lorenz calls such display signals "the language of animals."

Figure 4–1. Female lark sparrow on the nest. The nesting of birds is a phenological event—a periodic biological phenomena. The lark sparrow is one of the most attractive birds of the open country. It is a common species in the Midwest but does not occur east of the Allegheny mountains.

There are several different types of display. One is called *threat display* and takes place between rival males. It involves the defense of home territories (see Chapter 5).

Any type of display that brings the male and female together and leads to copulation is called *epigamic display* (from the prefix *epi*, meaning upon, and the Latin word *gamic*, meaning requiring fertilization). Epigamic display occurs during courtship.

Postnuptial display (from the prefix *post*, meaning after, and the word *nuptial*, meaning marriage) is any display between nesting pairs. This type of bird display presumably keeps the pair-bond intact during incubation and care of the fledgling.

Although Konrad Lorenz calls such display signals the language of animals, he does not mean that birds actually talk and reason with each other as do human beings. Bird display signals are *innate*. Complicated display signals are understood between the individuals of a species without any previous learning experience. The signals are automatic and almost mechanical in nature. The most familiar of all bird display signals is the spring songs of birds. Although we do not often think about it, we are so familiar with many of these display songs that we label the singer a "song bird."

The displays performed by most birds during courtship are quite involved. We know very little about the series of display signals that finally leads to the pair-bond in most species. More will be said about display in Chapter 9.

HOW BIRDS MATE

Display patterns during courtship lead to *copulation* between the sexes. Copulation is the joining of male and female to transfer sperm from the *cloaca* of the male to the cloaca of the female. The cloaca is the common chamber into which the intestinal, urinary, and reproductive canals of birds and reptiles empty. The transfer of sperm is accomplished by the male bird balancing on the back of the female and pressing the edge of his cloaca against hers.

The reproductive tracts of a male and female passerine bird are shown in Figures 4–2 and 4–3.

The drawings are of the bird's reproductive tract during the breeding season. This reproductive tract varies tremendously in size depending on the season of the year. The testes of a breeding male may enlarge from hundreds to thousands of times depending on species. The female organs also enlarge as the *ova* (eggs) mature in the ovaries.

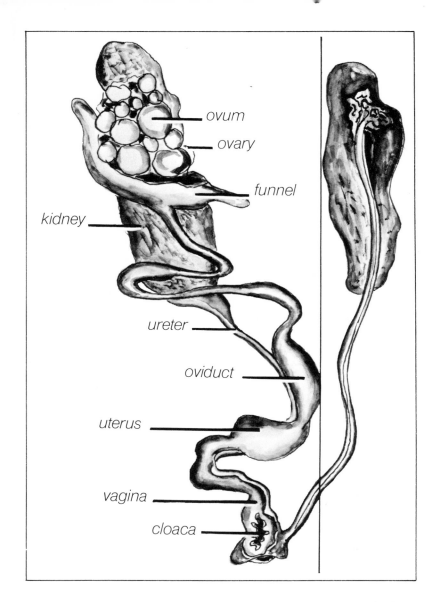

Figure 4–2.   The female reproductive system. As in the male the kidney and ureter are behind the reproductive organs. The ovum (yolk of the egg) moves from the ovary into the funnel, and down the oviduct where fertilization takes place. The egg albumen (egg white) is produced in the oviduct. The shell membrane and shell are formed in the uterus and the egg deposited from the cloaca. The process of passage of the egg through the oviduct takes about one day. The reproductive organs of the female are also paired, but in most birds only the left ovary is functional. The right ovary is rudimentary. In some falcons and hawks, however, there are two functional ovaries as shown here. The right ovary is depicted in the breeding condition and the left ovary in the reduced (eclipse) nonbreeding condition.

PHOTOPERIODISM

The change in the *gonads* (sex organs) of a bird as it approaches breeding season is a phenological event, as much so as the flowering of plants in the spring or the dropping of leaves in the fall. One of the most important climatic factors controlling migration and breeding is light. Scientists call the alternating periods of lightness and darkness as they effect the growth and maturity of a living organism the *photoperiod.* Photoperiodism is the capacity of an organism to respond to various time lengths of light and darkness. The amount of light that an organism receives varies with the length of the day as the seasons change. Scientists study the effect of photoperiodism in organisms by varying the light (day) and dark (night) cycle in large temperature- and light-control chambers. Since temperature also affects the life cycles of living things, temperature in the chambers is recorded.

Eighteenth- and nineteenth-century ornithologists believed that the regulation of the breeding cycles of birds was mainly a temperature phenomenon. This, of course, was a logical assumption because birds migrate to warmer climates as the cold weather approaches. Within the last few decades, however, the physiological response of birds to varying amounts of light has also been studied. Now we know that light is much more important to the timing of reproductive processes than temperature.

Dr. C. M. Weise studied the gonadal response of white-throated sparrows, slate-colored juncos, and fox sparrows to long and short day lengths. He kept these species in a light chamber for eighteen months under a continuous nine-hour day and fifteen-hour night (9 L–15 D), in a light and dark regime designed to simulate long periods of short winter days. He found that the gonads did not increase in size.

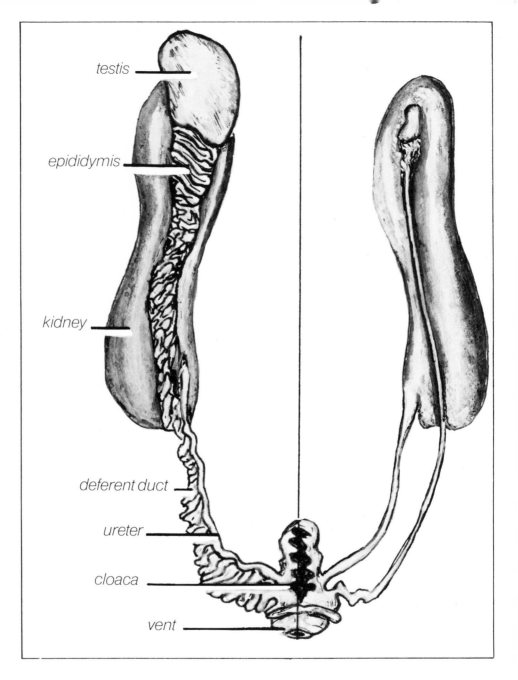

testis

epididymis

kidney

deferent duct

ureter

cloaca

vent

Figure 4–3.   Reproductive organs of a male bird. The organs are paired. The kidney and ureter (excretory duct for the urine) are behind the reproductive organs. The sperm from the testis and epididymis move down the deferent duct (sperm duct) to the cloaca. During sperm transfer mating birds press the edges of the cloaca together. The right testis is depicted in the breeding condition and the left testis in the reduced (eclipse) nonbreeding condition.

The birds' migratory response, a restlessness called *Zug-unruhe* (from the German *zug*, meaning flight, and *unruhe*, meaning restless), was also suppressed. *Zugunruhe* of the juncos and fox sparrows was delayed by two months, while the white-throated sparrows failed to exhibit any migratory response at all.

When Dr. Weise reversed the light cycle (15L–9D), he found that the testes increased from the nonbreeding size of 2–5 milligrams in weight to 200–300 milligrams, which is the breeding size. The female ovaries went from 3–8 milligrams to 30–50 milligrams, which is normal for the female as she approaches *ovulation* (egg formation).

From experiments such as these we know that the amount of light during the seasons has a profound effect on the breed-

Figure 4–4. Male white-throated sparrow feeding fledgling. Fledgling birds usually have different and more subdued coloring than the adult male.

ing biology of birds. Unfortunately there still has been very little work done on the effect of the kind of light involved. The light spectrum consists of complex wave lengths, each with a different frequency. White light is made up of wave lengths from 0.4–0.7 micrometers long (1 micrometer = 1/1000 of a millimeter). Each color is a different wave length: blue, for instance, is 0.4 micrometers, green, 0.5 micrometers, red, 0.65 micrometers long. The sun also produces infrared and ultraviolet light besides the visible light that our eye is tuned to. Both the sun and a light bulb give off more infrared light than visible light. What is the effect of infrared or ultraviolet light on the breeding cycle of birds?

MOLTING

Fledglings that have left the nest and birds that are not sexually mature are often colored differently from adult birds. Warblers that are migrating are often quite difficult to identify, for during their first year the young birds do not resemble the adults. The immature parula warbler, for instance, has a dull olive-gray back and indistinct wing bars. The adults have bluish backs with very distinct wing bars.

The adult sharp-shinned hawk, both male and female, is a beautifully colored slate-blue bird with white underparts heavily barred with reddish brown. Its eyes are bright red. First-year immature birds are brown above and streaked with brown or black below. They have yellow eyes. Unless one knows the shape of the hawks—a small hawk with short, rounded wings and a long tail—the young and adult might be mistaken for different species. The colors of immature birds usually change after the first molt.

Birds molt all of their feathers. Only a few feathers are dropped at a time over an extended period, because if birds

Figure 4-5. White ibis feeding. The mature white birds can be seen behind the first-year immature birds which are in the foreground. The first-year birds are colored a dull grayish brown. They frequent low, moist ground around lakes where they feed mainly on small crustaceans such as crawfish.

shed all of their feathers at once, they could not fly. The patterns of dropping feathers vary from species to species. The annual molt that takes place each year is called postnuptial molt because it usually takes place after the breeding season. Michael P. Harris of Oxford University, England, studied the swallow-tailed gull on the Galapagos Islands and found that most adult gulls began the replacement of their primary flight feathers at the time the young left the nest. There were exceptions, however, and a few individuals began replacement of the innermost primaries as the eggs hatched.

Small birds, such as warblers, may lose all of their tail feathers at once. Apparently they can fly well enough without them. Most large birds, however, especially birds of prey, lose their tail feathers in pairs. If a sharp-shinned hawk, for instance, lost all of its tail feathers at one time, it would be

Figure 4–6. The little blue heron has the exact opposite color phases as the white ibis. The adult bird is a slate-blue color like the great blue heron, but the first-year immature bird is pure white. This picture demonstrates how large birds such as herons and hawks lose their feathers in pairs when they molt. Pairs of the juvenile white feathers still remain in the primary and secondary wing feathers of this young heron. It has almost reached the mature slate-blue color.

severely handicapped. It hunts in thick woods and uses its tail as an efficient rudder. Without the tail it would not be able to twist and dodge through thick brush and catch its prey.

SEXUAL MATURITY

The age at which birds reach sexual maturity differs considerably. Our national emblem, the stately bald eagle, does not reach maturity for three years. Bald eagles obtain their beautiful adult plumage, the white head and tail feathers, at the end of the third annual molt. They do not usually mate and breed until they are four to six years old.

Small birds, such as sparrows, doves, and woodpeckers, begin nesting activities during the first spring season after they leave the nest. They may be less than a year old. Most hawks and owls, sea gulls, geese, and larger birds begin breeding the second year after leaving the nest. Ornithologist J. D. Ligon, who studied the breeding biology of the uncommon red-cockaded woodpecker near Gainesville, Florida, found that most of these birds, especially the males, do not breed at one year of age. First-year females, however, become independent sooner than the males and often breed the first year, wandering until they find an unmated male in possession of a territory. Since the young remain with their parents until the following spring, the males have little opportunity to locate a tree with dead heartwood suitable for excavation or time to set up a territory. A suitable nesting site and feeding and nesting territory must be established before the male can successfully form a pair-bond with a free female woodpecker. Reproduction in birds follows a complex series of behavioral patterns, and mating success is dependent on the completion of each part of the overall pattern.

5. Nests and Nesting

THE OBSERVATION OF NESTING BIRDS AND BREEDING BEHAVIOR is not a modern pastime, for the home life of birds has always intrigued people. Observing bird life at the nest is a fascinating way to study breeding biology. There is no substitute in the science of ornithology for the direct observation of birds. As long ago as the thirteenth century Frederick II watched the nests of herons, falcons, and vultures. He was a careful student of bird life and drew correct conclusions from his observations, unswayed by the popular misconceptions of his time. He rejected the myth that European barnacle geese were hatched from barnacles on trees. He dissected barnacles, and, seeing nothing that resembled a goose, he concluded the story had spread because no one knew where the geese bred. We know now that the barnacle goose breeds in colonies on ledges of steep Arctic cliffs along the rocky river gorges, but no medieval European writer knew its nesting site.

Egg collecting, especially during childhood, has led many individuals to the study of birds. Egg collecting is not to be recommended, however, for it destroys nests. Fortunately, it is only the common birds that suffer losses to inquisitive young bird watchers. The Audubon Society has educated the public so that nest watching rather than egg collecting is the pastime of young naturalists. The professional adult collector is still a menace to bird life because he seeks out the more rare species.

Lt. Col. W. H. Sleeman in his fascinating book, *Rambles and Recollections* (1844), points out the basic difference in the philosophies of East and West toward bird nests. On one of his journeys he passed close to an Indian village where children were playing and describes the scene:

> Upon the bushes over their heads were suspended an immense number of beautiful nests of the Baya bird, or Indian yellowhammer, all within reach of a grown-up boy, and one so near the road that a grown-up man might actually look into it as he passed along, and could hardly help shaking it. It cannot fail to strike a European as singular, to see as many birds nests, situated so close to a village, remain unmolested within reach of so many boisterous children.

He goes on:

> With us it is different—to discover birds nests is one of the first modes in which a boy exercises his powers, and displays his love of art. Upon his skill in finding them he is willing to rest his first claim to wisdom and enterprise. His trophies are his string of eggs.

With time the Western attitude is changing. The modern student of birds can obtain a far better trophy than eggs with camera and film. The high-power telephoto lens is an efficient and not excessively expensive piece of equipment. However, even without high-power lens equipment good bird portraits can be obtained. I took some of my first photographs of nest-

ing birds with an inexpensive Jiffy Kodak when I was four-
teen years old. A few are in this book. How much more satis-
fying to have a picture of a living bird rather than a useless
dead egg!

WHY BIRDS BUILD NESTS

Birds have evolved from reptiles. The body of a reptile is
covered with scales, as are the legs of birds. This is a visible
indication that birds had ancient reptilian ancestors. Reptiles,
however, are cold-blooded animals: their blood temperature
varies with the temperature of the environment, and they tol-

Figure 5–1.   Reptiles are the ancestors of birds. Birds and reptiles
lay eggs and like reptiles, birds have scales, although only on the
legs and feet. Archaeopteryx is the earliest known bird. In bone
structure, it resembled a tiny dinosaur, but it had feathers. The
tail feathers grew from a long slender tail like a lizard tail. The
beaklike jaws were armed with teeth. The archaeopteryx fossils
were found in the limestone beds from the Upper Jurassic period
(135 to 180 million years ago) in Bavaria.

Figure 5–2. The barred owl nests in hollows in large trees. The nest of this young owl is under the hands of the Boy Scout holding it. Most species of owls nest in hollow trees.

erate tremendous variations in blood temperature. The temperature of birds, like that of mammals, is regulated and must remain constant regardless of variation in outside air temperature. The same is true for the embryo in the egg.

In almost all cold-blooded reptiles, eggs are hatched by the sun or the heat of decaying material. Turtle eggs are covered with sand, and snakes bury their eggs in decaying organic matter. As the physiology of birds evolved toward a warm-blooded metabolism, it became necessary to develop a system for the protection of the egg. The sun could not be depended upon to hatch the egg. Excessive cold would kill the warm-blooded embryo.

The evolution of birds from cold-blooded creatures to warm-blooded ones had a tremendous effect on their behavior.* It was the most important step in their evolution, even

*For a better understanding of evolutionary processes see *The Evolution of Insects* by the author.

Figure 5–3.   Nest of killdeer in a strawberry patch. The killdeer, like the common tern, has splotched eggs that blend well with the ground. The nest is a few pebbles and small sticks scooped together to make a hollow. The hatched young is even better camouflaged than the egg. Can you see it? Beautiful eggs such as these are a temptation to collectors.

more so than flight or the development of feathers. It led to the complex behavior of nest building and incubation necessary for the protection of the embryo within the egg.

INCUBATION

Incubation is the process by which birds supply heat from their own bodies to keep the egg at a constant temperature. In most birds incubation begins after all the eggs are laid. That is why all young birds in a nest are the same size. There are, of course, exceptions. Owls begin incubation as soon as the first egg is laid, so a nest of owls may contain three or four different-sized young. The young from the last egg is the "runt" of the nest and usually has a difficult time competing for food with its larger brothers and sisters. More often than not it dies or is pushed out of the nest. This is an especially common occurrence among eagles as well as owls.

After the eggs are laid and the time for incubation approaches, the female develops a *brood patch* on her breast. It is a bare area where the skin becomes suffused with blood. Birds turn their eggs at least twice a day to keep all the parts of the egg in contact with the warm brood patch. As a general rule (but there are exceptions) if both the male and female are colored alike, they share the incubation duties. If they are colored differently, like the brightly colored male cardinal and dull brown female, then only the female incubates the eggs.

Among the red-cockaded woodpeckers, incubation is performed by both parents and begins before the whole clutch of eggs is complete. The male remains on the nest at night, and the male and female take turns during the day. The clutch size is usually four, but since incubation begins as soon as the eggs are laid and they hatch at different times, the nest

Figure 5–4. Large birds such as magpies, crows, hawks, and herons use heavy sticks to construct their nests. This magpie nest is almost like a fortress. Magpie nests are covered with a roof of heavy sticks and usually have an entrance on one side and a smaller escape exit on the opposite side. During the nesting season the long tail of the mother bird can usually be seen sticking out of the entrance hole.

Figure 5–5. Red-cockaded woodpecker at its nesting cavity. This woodpecker has become rare in the South. It is usually limited to stands of mature or overmature pine, where it excavates its nesting cavity in old, diseased pine trees. PHOTO BY KIRTLEY-PERKINS.

hardly ever produces more than two fledglings. The last two usually starve to death and are thrown out of the nesting hole. (Although hatching rate is high for such birds, the number of fledglings that survive is only 50 percent.)

THE SIZE OF THE NEST

The size of a nest depends on the size of the bird. The nest of a bald eagle may be as large as six feet across, while a hummingbird's nest may be only slightly larger than a fifty cent piece.

Francis H. Herrich of Western Reserve University observed a bald eagle nest near Vermillion, Ohio, that was occupied continually for thirty-five years. It was built eighty-five feet above the ground in a shell-bark hickory and measured twelve feet in height and eight and one-half feet across the top. After it fell, it was estimated to weigh at least two tons.

WHERE BIRDS NEST

Some birds do not build a nest at all. The killdeer lays its eggs right on the ground, usually in an open field with small plants for cover. One nest I photographed was in a strawberry patch.

Generally the larger bird is the more likely to nest high up in the trees. Most of the common song birds and smaller birds, such as warblers, nest lower down, from two to fifteen feet above the ground in small trees or bushy cover. The nesting place of each species depends to a great extent on its feeding habits and the habitat to which it has adapted. The ovenbird, for instance, is a warbler, but it nests on the ground. Unlike most warblers it does not glean its food from the

Figure 5–6. The brown kiwi of New Zealand. The flightless kiwi probably was an early offshoot of the ostrich evolutionary line. The kiwi has managed to survive in spite of the reduction of forest lands in New Zealand. They now inhabit semicleared scrub country where they nest among dense vegetation in deep burrows. Incubation of the one large egg takes seventy-five to eighty days. The long hairs around the face are modified feathers called tacticle bristles. Kiwi have weak eyesight and the long feather bristles enable them to move about at night in the darkness of thick undergrowth. The long bill probes in the ground for worms and insect larvae.

leaves and limbs of trees but rather from the forest floor. It searches the ground, turning over leaves and leaf mold for small insects, snails, slugs, spiders, and other such creatures.

The nest is almost always located in open areas on the forest floor. The ovenbird prefers to build its nest alongside trails or woodland roads in the partially cleared areas where some sunlight filters through. The Cooper's hawk, which nests from twenty-five to fifty feet up in the trees and builds a large, flat stick nest, also prefers to build in thick woods along the edge of open trails, roads, or clearings. It is possible that the open areas are advantageous to forest birds approaching the nest. If one is familiar with the behavior patterns of nesting birds, then it is easy to locate their nests.

WHAT NESTS ARE MADE OF

The ovenbird nest is a delicate creation of dry grasses, vegetable fibers, leaves, weed stems, rootlets, and hairlike fibers that tie it together. In pine woods it is often constructed mainly of pine needles. It is built in a slight depression in

Figure 5–7.   Osprey nest. Birds sometimes use man-made structures to support their nests. This osprey nest near Cedar Key, Florida, sits atop a power pole. PHOTO BY THELMA CARLYSLE.

Figure 5–8. Nest of the Montezuma orpendola of Central America. This bird is known as the giant oriole or hangnest in Costa Rica. Like its relative, the Baltimore oriole, it constructs a very complex hanging nest. The giant orioles of Central America are large crow-sized birds. Their large basketlike nests hang from the tips of the fronds of tall palm trees.

the ground and covered with dead leaves and small fallen branches. Its resemblance to a rounded Dutch oven gives the bird its name.

Small birds such as the robin may take six or seven days to construct a nest. At the other extreme is the magpie, which may take two and one-half to three months to build its large, bulky nest. Large birds such as crows, magpies, hawks, and herons use heavy sticks to construct their nests. Nicolaas A. M. Verbeek of Redpath Museum, McGill University, Montreal, found that on cold days nest-building activities of the yellow-billed magpie are reduced. At temperatures between 43° and 52° F. a pair brought 41 sticks to the nest from 7:30 A.M. to 4:00 P.M. The next day when the temperature dropped to 40° they carried only 13 sticks to the nest. The finished nest contained 1,573 sticks and weighed 11,270 grams.

The red-cockaded woodpecker excavates cavities in living pines that are infected with a fungal disease called red heart. The disease attacks the heartwood of trees and causes it to break down. It is a disease of old age in pines so that the red-cockaded woodpecker is limited to woods of mature and over-mature pines. There are few such forests left in the South, so the distribution of this woodpecker is severely limited.

Birds that live in reed ponds, swamps, and grassy margins of lakes usually build their nests from cattails or dead reeds raised above the water on a bed of decaying rushes. The nest of the least bittern is a compact platform of plant stems and grasses, situated in bunches of tall cattails, grasses, or tall reeds from one to three feet above the water. In Florida the least bittern often chooses a cattail pond covered with a thick growth of buttonwood bushes.

The smooth-billed ani, which breeds in south Florida, nests in communes. Several breeding pairs build a common nest in which two or more adults lay their eggs. All the adults share the incubation and feeding of the nestlings.

The flightless, nocturnal kiwi of New Zealand nests in long burrows in the ground. The nesting burrow may be as long as eight and one-half feet and contains one egg. The kiwi egg is enormous and has an incubation period of seventy-five days. There are three species of kiwis. In the species that lives on the North Island of New Zealand the male bird undertakes all duties of incubation and care of the chick. Chick kiwis are not fed by the parents but fend for themselves as soon as they hatch.

Some birds build extremely complex nests. The weaver birds of Africa build highly organized nests. Weaving requires flexible materials which can be maneuvered by the bird. The male begins the nest by weaving a ring which he stands in while he finishes the globular nest. He pokes and vibrates the strips of plant material to bind twigs. He reverses the direction of windings between side-by-side twigs and pokes and pulls the end of long strips through a hole made by looping the strips.

When the meshwork becomes too close together to weave, the male thatches a roof within the overhead strips. He does not complete the entrance tube to the nest, however, until after a female accepts it. Once she has accepted the nest, she prevents the male from entering it again. The fine interior work is done by the female. While the female incubates the eggs, the male strengthens the nest and smoothes and compacts the outside to give it a neat appearance.

These are but a few examples of the variation of nest building among species of birds. A nest may be as simple as the depression in the sand of the common tern or as complex as the woven nest of the weaver birds.

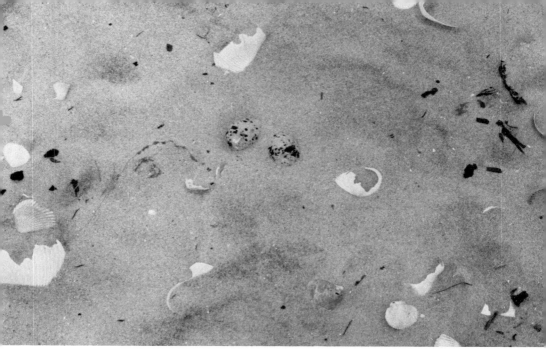

Figure 5–9. Nests of the common tern, which hardly bothers to build a nest but lays its eggs on the bare sand. It is careful, however, to lay them among bits of beach debris. The dark spotted eggs are well hidden among the white seashells and dark bits of surrounding driftwood. These eggs were found by the author on Cumberland Island, Georgia, which will become a national wilderness area. The average person does not realize how such simple pastimes as collecting seashells and driftwood may affect the home life of a bird species. Clean bathing beaches are not usually occupied by terns.

6. Of Home and the Weather: Where Birds Live

THE HOME OF A BIRD OR OTHER LIVING ORGANISM IS CALLED its habitat. A habitat is the place where a plant or animal species naturally lives and grows. It contains all the physical features, such as soil, weather, and food, normally preferred by a biological species. Of course, the habitat may vary from time to time in the life cycle of a bird. The winter habitat of a migrating species is considerably different from the summer habitat. As we pointed out in the first chapter, the feeding and nesting habitats may also be different, although in most species they are in the same area or very close together.

The habitat of a bird is a part of its ecological niche. Several species of birds may live in a single habitat and still have different ecological niches. The nesting habitat of the kingfisher and the bank swallow is the borders of streams. Both species nest in burrows excavated in the gravel or clay banks. Although their nesting habitat is the same, they have different feeding requirements.

The kingfisher feeds in streams, taking small fish from the water. The bank swallow takes its food from the air above the surface of the water. It twists and zigzags down the stream feeding on airborne insects. The large, self-reliant fisherman lives on good terms with its little, insect-hunting neighbor. They do not compete with each other for the same food. The feeding habitat of both is the stream, but they do occupy different feeding niches in that habitat.

In a single area many species of birds may occupy a certain habitat. If they each fill different ecological niches, however, they will not compete for food and shelter with one another. Their niches all interlock in time and space, and

Figure 6–1. The habitat of the long-legged limpkin is the swamps and lowland cypress forests along the edges of Florida waterways. During early spring and summer limpkins haunt the swampy shores in search of large freshwater snails found in the shallows. To local people they are known as "crying bird" because of the melancholy sadness of their call. PHOTO BY KEVIN CALLAHAN.

Figure 6–2. Nest of the limpkin. In the swamps along the Oklawaha River, stumps from cut-over timber are abundant. The
stumps are covered with vines and brush. Atop these vine-clad
pillars the secretive crying bird lays its four to seven eggs. The
next is a shaggy affair of dead vines, grass, moss, and other kinds
of vegetation. In spite of its restricted habitat, the limpkin is holding its own in Florida. The large population along the Oklawaha
was saved by the decision to stop the cross-Florida barge canal.

together they fit like pieces of a puzzle into the overall ecological picture of the region.

Aretas A. Saunders of the New York State Museum in Al-
bany counted the bird species that inhabited a 503-acre oak-
hickory forest in southern New York. He observed 26 different species in this plant habitat (see Table 6–1).

If we study Mr. Saunders's bird list and learn the habitats
of the various species of birds, then we can understand how
the separate niche of each species fits it into the single oak-
hickory habitat. In other words, we get an overall picture of
the bird community of the habitat.

We must break down the list into several different feeding

TABLE 6–1

Birds of a New York Mature Oak-Hickory Forest

SPECIES	AVERAGE PER 100 ACRES	TOTAL NUMBER OF BIRDS
Red-eyed vireo	15.4	77
Ovenbird	14.6	73
Black-throated green warbler	12.4	62
Black-throated blue warbler	10.3	52
Magnolia warbler	9.2	46
Black and white warbler	8.6	43
Wood thrush	7.4	37
Wood pewee	5.6	28
Chickadee	4.6	23
Flicker	4.4	22
Junco	4.2	21
Crow	4.1	20
Scarlet tanager	3.8	19
Blue jay	3.7	18
White-breasted nuthatch	3.1	16
Hairy woodpecker	2.7	13
Redstart	2.1	11
Hooded warbler	1.4	7
Blackburnian warbler	1.3	6
Hermit thrush	1.2	6
Red-tailed hawk	.9	4
Ruffed grouse	.9	4
Screech owl	.4	2
Barred owl	.2	1
Red-shouldered hawk	.2	1
All species (26)	126.6	612

and nesting categories. Starting from the forest floor we find the ovenbird, wood thrush, junco, hermit thrush, and ruffed grouse. All of these species nest and feed at ground level.

The two most common species in the list are both insectivorous. Most of the food of the red-eyed vireo, especially during

Figure 6–3.   Hermit thrush. The habitat of the hermit thrush is the damp forest floor of the eastern United States and Canada. It winters in the southern United States. Its food is about 50 to 60 percent animal matter gleaned from the forest floor. The song of the hermit thrush is one of the most beautiful of the bird world. It is a never-to-be-forgotten clear flutelike melody. A fitting local name is the American nightingale.

Figure 6–4. The black-crowned night heron. This heron feeds chiefly in the twilight. Although it nests in colonies, it is solitary when hunting the edges of shallow tidal creeks in flood plain habitats. It may nest in a colony miles from its feeding grounds. Thus the feeding and nesting habitats are well separated in this species.

the nesting season, consists of caterpillars and moths. The destructive gypsy moth and the tent caterpillar are favorite foods of the useful little vireo. As we have seen in Chapter 5, the ovenbird feeds on spiders, slugs, ants, and small ground-dwelling insects. The ovenbird does not compete with the tree-dwelling red-eyed vireo, but what of all the tree-dwelling warblers on the list? Most of the warblers consume insects, yet they are still separated to a certain extent in different niches.

The black and white warbler nests close to the ground, usually at the base of a stump or in hidden crevices behind roots or windfalls. It gleans its insect food from bark. Click beetles and bark insects are picked from behind slabs of bark.

The magnolia warbler, which is on the list, feeds on plant lice, beetles, and flies. It builds its nest one to fifteen feet above the ground in spruce or hemlock trees. Spruce and hemlock are usually a part of a maple-beech-hemlock forest, but hemlock trees may also be found near oak-hickory forests, especially on the slopes of cool, moist ravines. The magnolia warbler uses both plant communities for its aphid hunting, and thus it overlaps with the habitat of the other warblers.

The magnolia warbler is an example of how the common names of birds can be completely misleading. The magnolia tree is found only in the South, and yet the warbler is a northern bird of the Canadian forests and never nests south of the mountains of North Carolina. It was first described by the great early American ornithologist Alexander Wilson, who shot one out of a magnolia tree in Mississippi. It was no doubt on its way to its winter grounds in Central America. The accident of its being shot out of a magnolia tree left it with a misleading common name.

The woodpeckers on the list take care of the bark and wood-boring insects, while the crows and blue jays fill the niche of generalized feeders. Even the birds of prey have separate niches in the same oak-hickory habitat. The large red-tailed hawk nests in the woods but does its hunting over the open fields where it catches the larger rodents. The nest of the smaller red-shouldered hawk is most likely to be found along moist ravines where it can catch frogs, small snakes, salamanders, and forest-dwelling mice.

Owls, of course, hunt at night and are separated from the niche of the day-hunting hawks by time. The barred owl lives mainly on mice, frogs, and crawfish but catches them in the densest growth of forest trees. The screech owl, on the other

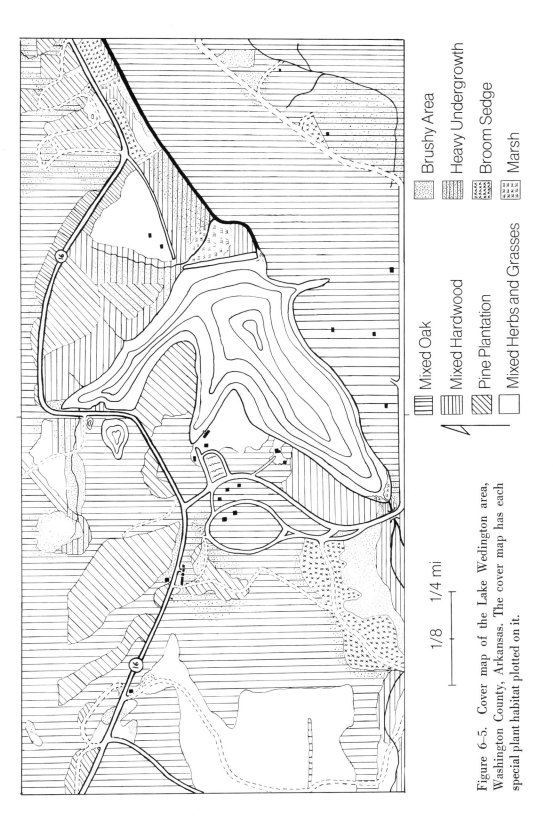

Brushy Area

Heavy Undergrowth

Broom Sedge

Marsh

Mixed Oak

Mixed Hardwood

Pine Plantation

Mixed Herbs and Grasses

1/8   1/4 mi

Figure 6–5. Cover map of the Lake Wedington area, Washington County, Arkansas. The cover map has each special plant habitat plotted on it.

hand, feeds on both mice and insects. It tends to hunt in more open areas than the barred owl.

Some birds on the list, such as the ruffed grouse, live mainly on vegetable food, although the young eat ground-dwelling insects. The grouse diet includes a large range of fruits, seeds, mast (accumulations of acorns and nuts), acorns, beechnuts, sumacs, and other plant material.

The habitat of all of these birds is linked closely to the food requirements of each species. Each species harvests a crop from the diverse plant community in which it lives.

COVER MAPPING THE HABITAT

One way to study the habitat of birds is to make a cover map of a region. A cover map is a map of the various types of plant communities in an area. Figure 6–5 is a cover map of two square miles of an upland Ozark plateau. For one full year I studied the bird population of this wooded, hilly terrain in the northwestern corner of Arkansas.

To begin my map, I broke down the plant cover into seven different types of plant communities. I found that scrubby stands of mixed oak species covered 61 percent of the hilly upland area. The second largest plant community consisted of lowland flood plain species. Such trees as sycamore, river birch, black willow, sweet gum, water locust, bodark, sassafras, red bud, and buttonbrush occupied low areas near the lake and along streams. Scattered among these lowland and highland communities were plantings of pines, open areas of low herbs and grasses, overgrown bushy areas, woods with heavy undergrowth, and marshy areas near the lake.

By scouting each of these plant cover communities for certain fixed time periods each week, I was able to identify 135 species of birds. Of the 135 species, 69 were summer breeders

TABLE 6–2
Coefficient of Community between
Four Wedington Habitats

	FLOOD PLAIN (MIXED HARDWOOD)	MIXED OAK	FIELD AREAS	PINE PLANTATIONS
Flood Plain (Mixed Hardwood)	—	.36	.32	.25
Mixed Oak	.36	—	.21	.32
Field Areas	.32	.21	—	.27
Pine Plantations	.25	.32	.27	—

in the area, 18 were permanent, year-round, residents, 55 were transient species (migrating through), and 11 species were winter residents. A total of 35 families of birds was recorded with an average of 3.9 species per family utilizing the area.

By recording the number of birds observed per hour of observation, I calculated the relative abundance and frequency of occurrence for each species. The frequency of occurrence is given by the percentage of times that I observed each species out of the total number of scouting trips to each of the habitat communities.

The greatest number of species and individuals of each species occurred in the flood plain community. Although it composed only 10 percent of the study area, 57 percent of the species found occurred in it. The proximity to water, greater diversity of vegetation, and varied undergrowth made this the most heavily utilized habitat of the region. Although the upland oak region covered 61 percent of the total area (see cover map) only 37 percent of all species were found in that

TABLE 6–3

Frequency of Occurrence of Permanent Residents Observed on Weekly Trips in the Flood Plain Area

SPECIES	FREQUENCY OF OCCURRENCE (PERCENTAGE)	AVERAGE NUMBER PER HOUR OF OBSERVATION
Carolina chickadee	93.40	3.60
Crow	93.40	2.77
Cardinal	90.00	4.90
Blue jay	90.00	3.20
Flicker	56.60	.86
Carolina wren	43.40	.76
Tufted titmouse	43.40	.56
Downy woodpecker	33.40	.33
Red-bellied woodpecker	23.40	.40
Robin	13.30	.86
Hairy woodpecker	6.60	.10
Belted kingfisher	6.60	.06
Pileated woodpecker	6.60	.06
Bob white	3.30	.26

habitat. There is very little variety in such forests, and undergrowth is scanty. Less than 3 percent of the oak forest floor is covered with herbaceous scrubby plants. Tables 6–3, 6–4, and 6–5 show the frequency of occurrence for the bird species of the preferred flood plain habitat.

Table 6–6 gives the number of species and individuals of each species recorded for the five main Lake Wedington habitats. The least used of all the habitats was that formed by the pine plantings. Only eighty-one individuals of twenty-four species were recorded there during the entire period of the

TABLE 6–4

Frequency of Occurrence of Winter Residents Observed on Weekly Trips in the Flood Plain Area

SPECIES	FREQUENCY OF OCCURRENCE (PERCENTAGE)	AVERAGE NUMBER SEEN PER HOUR OF OBSERVATION
Cardinal	77.00	3.46
Blue jay	61.50	3.30
Carolina chickadee	61.50	2.00
Belted kingfisher	61.50	.69
Song sparrow	46.10	1.54
Crow	38.40	.69
Slate-colored junco	30.70	2.07
Flicker	30.70	.38
Downy woodpecker	30.70	.23
Wilson's snipe	23.00	.53
Tufted titmouse	23.00	.23
Carolina wren	23.00	.23
Robin	15.40	1.46
Bob white	15.40	1.30
Fox sparrow	15.40	.23
White-throated sparrow	7.70	.23
Red-tailed hawk	7.70	.23
Sharp-shinned hawk	7.70	.07
Pileated woodpecker	7.70	.07
Harris's sparrow	7.70	.07
Red-bellied woodpecker	7.70	.07

study. The accumulation of sterile needle layers under ever-
green forests makes a poor food supply. This raw, persistent,
and slowly decomposing accumulation of needles (called
"mor") was very abundant under the pine trees at Wedington. It provided no cover for ground-nesting birds, so the only
birds feeding in these stands were woodpeckers.

Counting the birds in different selected habitats is one
method we have to learn about density of bird life and where
birds live. Only a very small fraction of such bird habitats,
however, have been investigated by this method.

THE WEATHER

In Ireland, when the cold September winds begin to blow
from the west across Donegal, the small, streaked meadow
pipits leave the high moors moving south. Behind them several weeks later come the passage meadow pipits from Iceland, the Faroe Islands, and as far north as Greenland. The
delicate meadow pipits cannot withstand either severe arctic
or desert conditions. They move out of the icebound regions
in the winter and return to the north from the northern edge
of Africa during the summer drought. The northern passage
birds cross to the British Isles from Iceland and Greenland
and then stream south down both sides of the Irish Sea or
down the west coast of Ireland. The eastern birds from Scan-
dinavia cross to the coast of Scotland and follow the east
coast of England south. A few pipits remain in England for
the winter, but most cross to northern France where they mix
with pipits from Germany and the Low Countries. The gathering stream hugs the coast of France and Spain, eventually arriving in northwest Africa. Many pipits do not go all the way
to Africa but remain in the huge central area of Europe. Here
these migrating Arctic pipits mix with the year-round residents

Figure 6–6. The moorland habitat of the streaked meadow pipit. In Donegal County, Ireland, the cold September winds from the west bring the transient meadow pipit from as far north as Iceland and Faroe Islands. In the moorlands of western Ireland they stop and rest before continuing their long journey south to the northern edge of Africa.

of Europe. In this middle region resident pipits may move down a mountain side only a few hundred yards to escape the cold. Why do the passage meadow pipits migrate thousands of miles from the Arctic to North Africa while others remain stationary in central Europe? Behavior such as this is one of the fascinations of bird study.

We can speculate that perhaps the northern birds find more room and less competition for food in the north than in the milder middle regions. Most of them probably fly past the stationary middle population to Africa for this reason. It is obvious that the meadow pipit has an optimum temperature range and that its southern movement to new homelands is affected by temperature, winds, rainfall, and other climatic factors.

Weather affects a bird's food supply. The list (Table 6–3) of permanent residents of the flood plain habitat of Lake Wedington does not include any warblers or other totally insectivorous birds except woodpeckers. When cold approaches, insects die off or go into a form of hibernation called diapause. Winter snows cover the Ozark hills and make it very difficult for birds to find these diapausing insects. The five woodpecker species, of course, continue to get their insect food from inside trees. The blue jay and crow are scavengers, and the bob white is a ground-feeding seed eater. The cardinal is a great enemy of injurious insects in the summer, but it survives the winter quite well on plant material, particularly weed seeds.

The three little permanent winter residents, the Carolina chickadee, the Carolina wren, and the tufted titmouse, all have small, pointed beaks well-suited to collecting diapausing larvae or adult insects from the sheltered cracks and crevices of bark. The tufted titmouse is extremely agile and able to perform such acrobatic feats as hanging head downward to search twigs for its favorite food, insect eggs. It is also quite able to survive on berries, nuts, and acorns during the winter.

After most of the birds of the summer list (Table 6–5), such as the thrushes and warblers, have left for the warmer climes, and even the larger winter residents are reduced in numbers, this imp of the Ozark winter woodlands flits about in little flocks of five or six. When not in motion, searching the leafless trees along snow-covered banks, they snuggle close together for warmth in old nest holes. They are also one of the woodland birds that store up food when it is scarce. Few species of birds have so adapted for surviving the cold

TABLE 6–5

Frequency of Occurrence of Summer Residents Observed on Weekly Trips in the Flood Plain Area

SPECIES	FREQUENCY OF OCCURRENCE (PERCENTAGE)	AVERAGE NUMBER SEEN PER HOUR OF OBSERVATION
Carolina chickadee	69.23	2.62
Cardinal	61.54	2.23
Blue jay	61.54	2.31
Green heron	53.85	.77
Red-bellied woodpecker	53.85	.62
Crow	53.85	1.46
Belted kingfisher	46.15	.69
Phoebe	46.15	.92
Catbird	46.15	1.31
Field sparrow	46.15	2.77
Mourning dove	38.46	.54
Chimney swift	38.46	1.77
Red-winged blackbird	38.46	1.92
Blue grosbeak	38.46	1.00
Turkey vulture	30.77	1.23
Blue-gray gnatcatcher	30.77	1.15
White-eyed vireo	30.77	.46
Yellow-breasted chat	30.77	.54
Indigo bunting	30.77	.54
Barn swallow	23.08	.62
Brown thrasher	23.08	.31
Blue-winged warbler	23.08	.38
Prairie warbler	23.08	.46
Great blue heron	15.38	.15
Spotted sandpiper	15.38	.38

SPECIES	FREQUENCY OF OCCURRENCE (PERCENTAGE)	AVERAGE NUMBER SEEN PER HOUR OF OBSERVATION
Yellow-billed cuckoo	15.38	.38
Ruby-throated hummingbird	15.38	.31
Pileated woodpecker	15.38	.15
Wood pewee	15.38	.62
Tufted titmouse	15.38	.77
Carolina wren	15.38	.23
Wood thrush	15.38	.23
Red-eyed towhee	15.38	.31
Cowbird	15.38	.77
Red-eyed vireo	15.38	.15
Louisiana water thrush	15.38	.15
Kentucky warbler	15.38	.31
Cooper's hawk	7.69	.08
Broad-winged hawk	7.69	.15
Whip-poor-will	7.69	.08
Nighthawk	7.69	.62
Flicker	7.69	.08
Red-headed woodpecker	7.69	.08
Downy woodpecker	7.69	.15
Kingbird	7.69	.69
Mockingbird	7.69	.08
Robin	7.69	.38
Bluebird	7.69	.23
Black and white warbler	7.69	.08

weather. In the still of the winter woodlands or on a gray spring day, their loud, friendly "peto-peto-peto-peto-peto" is a welcome sound. It tells us to be happy with the weather the way it is, for spring is just around the corner!

TABLE 6–6

Species and Individuals Observed in Five Wedington Habitats

HABITAT	NUMBER OF		PERCENT OF TOTAL	
	Individuals	*Species*	*Individuals*	*Species*
Upland oak	409	43	17.2	37
Flood plain	1107	66	47.2	57
Grass areas	254	23	10.7	20
Lake edge and marsh	522	25	21.5	22
Pine plantations	81	24	3.4	21
Total	2373		100.0	

7. Bird Territories

IN 1886 A GERMAN ORNITHOLOGIST, BERNARD ALTUM, WROTE a book about bird behavior. He titled it *Der Vogel und Sein Leben*, which translates as *The Bird and His Life*. It might better have been titled *The Bird and His Land*. In a few pages of the study Altum first described his theory of bird territorialism. We all know that a territory is an area of land marked off by district boundaries, but what is a bird territory?

The first naturalists to observe bird behavior and to record it used such words as "jealousy" and "belligerence" to describe the bird fights that took place in their gardens. Zenodotus, an early Greek grammarian and editor in the third century B.C., wrote, "One bush does not shelter two robins." In 1772 Gilbert White wrote, "During the amorous season, such a jealousy prevails among male birds that they can scarcely bear to be together in the same hedge or field."

It is natural that these early bird watchers would believe that bird rivalry was a competition for the female. The eighteenth century was an age of romanticism, and people extended their own romantic fancy to nature. Bird songs were interpreted as love songs. Altum, however, disputed the theory of sexual rivalry and outlined his own hypothesis, which is still accepted as valid. He realized that bird conflicts were not over the female but that males were defending a plot of ground. The two parts of his theory stated first, that the male bird does not fight for the female but rather for possession of land, and second, that birds do not sing love songs but sing to warn off other bird intruders from their land domains.

In 1903 an Irishman, C. B. Moffat, in a paper published in the *Irish Naturalist* carried Altum's idea still further. He stated that not only do birds sing in order to frighten off intruders, but that the male's bright colors serve the same purpose.

The ideas of both Altum and Moffat were buried in the literature about birds and were little known to ornithologists of their own time. It remained for an English industrialist, Henry Elliot Howard, to resurrect the theory of territorialism and place it before science. Howard was a quiet, gentle businessman who spent his free time before breakfast each day bird watching. He kept detailed notes on his early morning rambles and in 1920 published a volume entitled *Territory in Bird Life*. This book holds the same place of honor among students of bird behavior as Darwin's *Origin of Species* does among evolutionists.* The essentials of his outline, with minor variations, are accepted by modern ornithologists.

According to Howard a territorial species can be recognized by certain definite characteristics. They are:

1. Males disperse and isolate themselves in spring.
2. They remain only in one area.

*See the author's work, *The Evolution of Insects*.

Figure 7–1. A robin will even declare war on a stuffed robin or a tuft of red feathers if it feels that its territory is being threatened.

3. They do not allow other males of the same species to intrude into their area and drive them off.
4. They announce the possession of their territory by song, while at the same time attracting a mate.

DR. LACK'S ENGLISH ROBINS

The English robin is a bold, neckless, little round ball of a bird about five inches long with a bright reddish-orange breast. If one walks along the edge of an English or Irish hedgerow, the bird most in evidence is this little red puffball that haunts the countryside. It flits from branch to branch and drops on doomed insects with a quick, impulsive dive. Even in the deep shadows of late evening its flashy red breast catches one's eye. The bird seems to have been designed by nature as a red flag to alert the senses.

Male and female robins are twins. In color, manners, and song they cannot be told apart. They defend and hold separate territories. There is no male chivalry, and they are very aggressive toward each other except for the short period of breeding and nesting. If the territories of a male and female adjoin each other, they are fused as one estate for breeding purposes. A truce is called and quiet reigns while family duties are discharged. The robin also remains unusually inconspicuous after the breeding season when molting takes place. As the summer progresses, however, warfare resumes. Each individual robin begins to sing within the boundaries of its own territory. The song usually warns other robins away.

If song fails, the trespasser is met with special robin signals of defiance. The outraged landowner is transformed into an image of fury. At the first sight of the intruder it stiffens and bobs up and down, then, as if triggered by a mysterious sign, it puffs out its brightly colored breast and moves it from side to side. If this warning fails, it attacks. With wings quivering it dashes across the lawn "tic, tic, ticking" at its opponent. The birds seldom meet in physical battle, for the usurper invariably departs in haste.

Dr. David Lack spent five years studying the behavior of the English robin. He discovered that the Irish ornithologist, C. B. Moffat, was correct and that the robin's brightly colored breast does serve as a warning signal. Dr. Lack designed some ingenious bird experiments. When he decided to study the life of the robin he trapped a few and placed them in a huge cage called an aviary. There was a hitch to his plan, however, for one of the male robins killed its four companions. There was no way in a closed aviary for them to escape the vicious attacks.

How could such a small bird be so deadly? The robin attacks species much larger than itself. Its beak is very slender, almost needle-like, and the robin uses it like a stiletto, thumping away at another bird with great accuracy. The usual point of attack is the back of the head at the base of the skull. This is a very vulnerable spot in vertebrate animals, for the spinal cord can be reached where the neck vertebrate meets the skull.

I made the same mistake as Dr. Lack with two magpies that I took from separate nests in Colorado. Magpies make interesting pets, and I thought it would be best to have two for companionship. I named them "Big Bird" and "Little Bird." For a short while things went well, but as spring approached Big Bird began attacking its companion. Big Bird became more and more belligerent and eventually would not even let Little Bird near the food dish or on the same perch. Over a two-month period "Little Bird" had all of his beautiful long tail feathers pulled out and became so raggedy looking that my daughter suggested that I rename him Raggedy Andy. I built a much larger cage in the back yard, but Big Bird still made life miserable for Little Bird and would not let him into his territorial corner of the cage. Finally a sort of poetic justice prevailed, and Big Bird died of some mysterious disease that I could not diagnose. Little Bird immediately began to change into a new being. He was no longer timid and jumpy. His beautiful tail feathers grew back, and he began preening and taking a daily bath, which he had not been allowed to do under the Big Bird regime.

My magpie now lives in happy freedom, chattering to himself and playing with eye-catching bright objects that take his fancy. He seems to have taken a new lease on life, happy to be free of Big Bird, the self-appointed dictator. It may be that

Big Bird never reached the point of killing Little Bird because, except during the nesting season, magpies are considered social birds. Social birds follow a behavioral pattern known as the *peck order*. Essentially, a peck order means that there is a hierarchy with a bold forceful leader and a long line of underlings arranged by rank from general down to private, each with certain privileges.

After his experience with caged birds Dr. Lack decided to return his research to the great outdoors. He experimented by placing stuffed birds of different colors in a robin's territory, and nothing happened. Whenever he put a stuffed robin in the territory of a living robin, however, total war was declared, and the stuffed robin was demolished. Before the attack, however, the robin threatened or bluffed the intruder bird by fluffing out its red breast and turning it slowly from side to side while facing the opponent. When Dr. Lack substituted a tuft of red feathers for a stuffed robin the same threatening display preceded any attack. It was rather humorous to see a full-grown live bird threatening tufts of feathers. The experiment proved to Dr. Lack's satisfaction that when the song of the robin failed to keep intruders out of its territory, then the next threat signal, the puffed-out red breast, succeeded. Not many robins get killed, for the threat display is an effective substitute for actual combat. The observant Irishman, C. B. Moffat, was correct about the color of birds being important to territorial behavior.

DR. YOUNG'S AMERICAN ROBINS

Dr. Howard Young of Wisconsin State University, La Crosse, Wisconsin, studied the territorial behavior of the American robin, one of our most familiar birds. It was named the robin by the early English settlers because of its reddish-

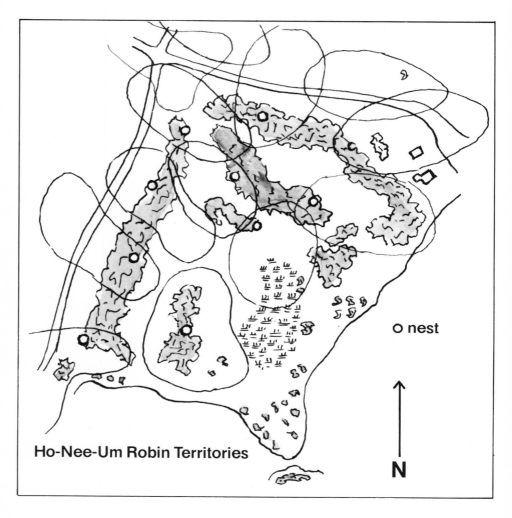

Figure 7–2.

orange breast. It is, in reality, a member of the thrush family and not related to the much smaller English robin.

Dr. Young observed robin behavior on 5.2 acres called the Ho-Nee-Um Pond area in Wisconsin. For three years he recorded in detail the behavior of all robins that utilized the area. He discovered when the first males arrived from the South and recorded their first songs and the first combat with other arriving males. In all he kept track of 204 robins.

In order to follow their individual lives, he had to trap and mark each bird. He marked them by coding each bird with different colored celluloid leg bands. There were so many robins, however, that he also had to color-code certain of their feathers. This was done by the falconer's technique of *imping*, a method of repairing broken feathers with sections of new feathers. He would cut off part of a feather, stick a pin down the hollow shaft, and slide a section of new, brightly colored feather over the pin, gluing it in place. An example would be a marked bird with a blue band on the right leg and a red band over a white band on the left leg. The tail would then have one outer tail feather imped, white on the left and red on the right side, to correspond to the red and white bands on the left leg. You can see what a very large number of birds could be marked and recognized by various color combinations. This was a big undertaking just to begin a behavioral experiment, for there was a tremendous amount of work involved in trapping and marking 204 robins. It was absolutely necessary, however, if Dr. Young was to do a thorough job of following the life histories and plotting the territories of enough birds for the experiment to be meaningful.

Such a research project illustrates the ends to which a scientist will go to insure that he collects enough data to reach sound conclusions. This is especially true in the study of the behavior of wild birds, which are always on the move.

TABLE 7–1

Spring Phenology for the Robin
At Ho-Nee-Um.

ACTIVITY	EARLIEST DATES			
	1947	1948	1949	Average
First males arrive	3/10	3/13	3/11	3/11
First song	3/23	3/16	3/22	3/20
First combat	3/28	3/21	3/23	3/24
First females arrive	3/20	3/21	3/26	3/23
First nesting starts	4/8	4/8	4/2	4/6

One of the most difficult problems to solve in behavioral research is a statistical one. The researcher must always try as best he can to determine what size sample of the population he must observe in order to obtain an overall view of behavior patterns. Obviously, he can never cover too large an area or keep track of all the birds, but if he observes too small a sample, he runs the risk of recording the exceptions rather than the true behavior patterns. Exceptions need to be recorded, but it is the normal overall behavior pattern of the species that counts. That is what good science is all about. Recordings of miscellaneous exceptions make good scientific footnotes but cannot tell us the real natural history of a species, whether it be human or bird.

What did Dr. Young learn for all his patience and labor? His results are found in thirty-seven pages entitled "Territorial Behavior in the Eastern Robin" published in the Proceedings of the Linnaen Society of New York. He concluded that American robins exhibit territorial behavior only in the spring and that they return to the same territory each year. The males arrive first and establish the territory, but the females, once mated, help to maintain the territory. Robins are usually successful in routing intruders but also tolerate a certain amount of intrusion. He described the threat posturing of the robin and showed that fighting was always associated with an area rather than with a particular bird. The boundary of the territory is fluid and may move in and out or even overlap another robin's territory. The success of robin fights fall off as the birds get farther and farther from the center of their territories.

Dr. Young's research showed that no definite line can be drawn between territorial and nonterritorial birds. For instance, the English robin defends a territory throughout most of the year, while the American robin is territorial only during the spring nesting season.

Many ornithologists believe that territorial behavior eliminates social hierarchies and the peck order, which most social birds set up. If my social magpies are any indication, however, then territorial behavior, which keeps individuals apart, must overlap with social behavior, in which birds set up hierarchies of dominant and underling birds and live together. Even in the territorial robin, the male dominates the female, which is a sexual peck order.

As I pointed out before, however, it is dangerous to draw conclusions from too small a sample. The territorialism of my two magpies was influenced by the fact that they were confined in a man-made cage. They are far too small a sample and may well represent the exception. Some Colorado student of magpie natural history might undertake an experiment like Dr. Young's with the robins and demonstrate that magpies are almost totally social birds with very little or no territorial behavior in their "magpie character."

The very fact that during my boyhood I counted 160 magpie nests very close together in a small wood along Cherry Creek near Denver, would indicate that they are more social than territorial. Perhaps that is why I thought that Big Bird and Little Bird would live together in harmony. That is the way science goes: our experiments never work out quite the way we think they should. It is always the exception that proves that rule!

8. Bird Defense:
To Live Another Day

WE HAVE DISCUSSED HOW A BIRD DEFENDS ITS TERRITORY against other birds of its own species. This is a special form of defense. Ornithologists have several different theories about why birds set up and defend a territory. Many ornithologists believe that it insures an adequate food supply for the young birds. Moffat believed that it serves as a sort of bird birth control and limits the size of a bird population. Both Moffat and Lack believed that it reduces competition for mates and nesting places. In other words, it allows the reproductive functions to proceed in an orderly fashion. One bird behaviorist, the Marquis of Tavistock, believed that territorialism spreads nesting birds apart and thus prevents epidemics of bird diseases through close contact. As Dr. Young points out, however, this later theory "flounders on those very rocks which support such large concentrations of sea birds."

There is another form of defense that is just as important as territorial defense: the bird must defend itself against predators. Birds make for good eating and are preyed upon both by bird predators and by four-legged predators.

The main predation of birds, other than by people of course, is carried on by those magnificent creatures, the birds of prey. We may include in this group two families: the Falconiformes—eagles, hawks, and falcons—and the Strigiformes—night-flying owls. It is extremely unfortunate that the early literature of American ornithology divided these groups into "good guys" and "bad guys," the "good guys" being the birds of prey that feed primarily upon such creatures as rats, mice, and insects and the "bad guys" being the bird-eating hawks and falcons.

Much of my life has been spent observing in the wild and training birds of prey for falconry. I have at one time or another owned and trained every species of North American eagle, hawk, and falcon except the osprey and bald eagle, which are fish eaters.

In my youth I was often upset when I read the literature of the National Audubon Society and, in fact, most bird literature. These writers invariably classified all the falcons, except the little kestrel, and the short-winged bird-eating hawks as damaging birds of prey. They did this in order to justify protecting the mice-eating hawks. Almost every bird club pamphlet would point out that the short-winged Cooper's hawk and sharp-shinned hawk, which feed primarily on other birds, do considerable damage but that the red-shouldered hawk and the red-tailed hawk should be protected at all costs because they eat mostly rats, mice, frogs, and snakes. This attitude is best labeled the gamekeeper mentality and is probably a holdover from our English heritage. The medieval English sportsman's love of birds of prey, based on the sport of falconry, changed to hatred after the arrival of the firearm. For some strange reason these so-called sportsmen, who took game with a gun, did not seem to be able to coexist with birds of prey. Gamekeepers shot or trapped hawks on sight.

Figure 8–1. Florida yellow rat snake capturing and swallowing a fledgling house sparrow. Such dramas are a part of the cycle of nature, and this picture should not be viewed anthropomorphically as a terrible tragedy. PHOTO BY GEORGE PERSON.

Figure 8–2. The eastern peregrine falcon, misnamed the duck hawk, is one of the most efficient bird predators on the wing. It feeds almost entirely on birds of all sizes. It is now extinct in the eastern part of its range. Ornithologists believe that excessive DDT in the environment caused the falcon to lay eggs with too thin eggshells. This bird is now on the endangered species list. It was also a victim of the European and American "gamekeeper" mentality that preached that the only good hawk was a dead hawk. It is the favorite hunting bird of falconers.

Even Professor Allen fell for the peculiar psychology. A picture in his book of the beautiful peregrine falcon is captioned, "Not all hawks are destructive, but here is a duck hawk feeding a fowl to its young." If one reads his book carefully, however, one feels that Dr. Allen did not really believe his own caption. He was too good an ecologist to think that any birds of prey are really destructive.

A fundamental ecological fact is that all birds of prey, in the overall view, are beneficial. The bird-eating hawks and falcons kill to live and in the process weed out the weaker individuals of species that they prey on. This is a process that contributes to what evolutionists and other biologists call "natural selection." It is summed up by that well-known phrase, "survival of the fittest." The weak, diseased, and slow individuals are captured, and the quick and the strong escape to breed and multiply. As for hawks taking chickens, good farmers keep their poultry in pens. Wildlife should not be penalized for the carelessness and stupidity of people.

HOW BIRDS ESCAPE

The best method of defense is, of course, escape by flight. When birds evolved wings they rose above the fangs of most ground predators. The ordinary house cat is perhaps the most efficient ground predator of birds. Lest we make the same mistake of condemning cats as we have hawks, we should remember that they also weed out the weak and unfit individuals. I have watched many a house cat stalking catbirds and mockingbirds in my back yard. In only one case have I seen a cat succeed. Most cat predation is probably on nestlings in the flight-learning stage. Nature compensates for the loss of nestlings, especially in ground-nesting birds, by a large clutch size. It is very doubtful if we can claim that the extinction of

Figure 8–3. Threat posture by a young great horned owl. When backed into a corner, young owls expand their feathers in this manner and hiss at the attacker. This type of threat posture is very impressive and must certainly intimidate an attacker.

any native birds has been brought about by predators, whether cats or hawks. However, humans have done a very good job on six or seven species.

Birds are sometimes caught by ground predators while they are absorbed in some feeding or reproductive activity. The prairie sharp-tailed grouse engages in a courtship duel in which the two males close their eyes tightly as if in a trance while drumming their wings. The duel ends when one gives a peep, arouses from the trance, and steals away. Sharp-tailed grouse often fall prey to the coyote while engaged in this peculiar trance-like courtship behavior.

The old English literature of falconry is filled with descriptions of the hairbreadth escapes of birds from hawks or falcons. One of the escape tactics of the skylark is to attempt to climb and remain above a high-flying falcon. Another description concerns magpie hawking in which a magpie trapped on the open prairie by a fast-flying hunting falcon reached the shelter of a barbed-wire fence post. It proceeded to circle the post, always keeping the post between itself and the falcon. The magpie would not fly even when the falconer walked up and picked it up. Needless to say the magpie was spared out of respect for its shrewd tactic.

In the experience of most observers strong, alert birds more often than not escape attacking raptors. Such attacks are a natural part of their day-to-day existence, and they resume their normal activities almost immediately.

INJURY FEIGNING

One of the most delightful escape techniques to watch is called injury feigning. We have all heard about the opossum and hog-nosed snake that play dead when captured. Sometimes birds also play dead. J. Couch in his book *Illustrations of Instinct* tells of a collector who caught a skylark in a butterfly net. When he grasped her, she felt limp and motionless as if dead. He threw the body away, and she fell to the ground like a stone. As she lay there, he pushed her body with his foot. After a short while the bird, trailing a wing, shuffled off as if her wing and legs had been broken. When she was far enough away, she took to the air in flight.

Playing dead is not as common as injury feigning. I have

observed this remarkable performance many times in widely separated species of different families. Once when I found the ground nest of a Kentucky warbler, the little bird ceased its probing among the leaves and trash of the damp earth and, feigning injury, attempted to lead me away from its helpless offspring. This type of behavior seems most often to involve protection of the nest of fledglings.

In a strawberry patch I located the nest of a killdeer. It could hardly be called a nest, for the camouflaged eggs lay on the bare ground, shaded by the horizontal leaves of a strawberry plant. The young had recently hatched, and I almost stepped on them. The mother, "killdeering" loudly, dragged herself helplessly between the rows of strawberries, one wing hanging limply and sweeping up puffs of dust as she led me away in desperate anguish. She was never less than thirty feet ahead of me. When, in her estimation, I had been led a sufficient distance from the fledglings, the killdeer actress swiftly recovered and flew off in a wide, sweeping circle.

It was all I could do to find the nest a second time, for the fledgling killdeers and the sandy earth are practically indistinguishable. I succeeded, however, and readied my camera for a repeat performance. I was soon rewarded with a second display of fakery that surpassed the original effort.

The most impressive example of injury feigning I have ever seen, I have never found described in a bird book. It came as a complete surprise to me that birds of prey should engage in such subterfuge. As a boy I climbed to the nest of a long-eared owl. It was located in a deep, white pine grove in New York. All winter I had watched the owls in the groves. I finally spotted the tail of the mother bird protruding from a large stick nest. As I climbed the tree, I expected to see the mother bird sail silently away when I approached the stick

platform. Instead she rolled over the edge of the nest and half
flying, half flopping fell or seemed to fall like a rock to the
carpet of pine needles below. Then, like the killdeer and the
warbler, she fairly struggled to her feet. Dragging one wing
and making the most violent contortions, she pulled herself
along the ground like a wounded pheasant. I had no sooner
climbed down when she flew off to the lower limb of a tall
pine tree and gazed solemnly at me as if she had no concern
whatsoever about my presence.

Investigations have shown that in many species injury
feigning becomes more common as the eggs get closer and
closer to hatching. The killdeer, if threatened, increases its

Figure 8–4.   Killdeer at the nest in a strawberry patch. The killdeer is a species that performs injury feigning to protect the
young. The nestlings of a killdeer are precocious for they can
walk and run as soon as they hatch. This is true of most ground-
nesting birds. Protective coloration also protects the young. Can
you see the hatched-out nestling below the mother's lifted foot?

effort of acting disabled each day of incubation. This behavior continues until the young are several days old. In most birds the behavior has been correlated with some phase of the reproductive cycle.

Some ornithologists have stated that injury feigning serves little purpose. This is an unfair judgment, for they are measuring its success on humans. Many observers have pointed out that it is a highly effective technique when performed for the benefit of raccoons and opossums, which are very fond of bird eggs. While man may not be fooled, he has evolved fairly late and is a reasoning creature. It is dangerous when attempting to find reasons for behavior patterns of animals to use human beings as a reference for scientific judgments. Thinking about lower forms of life as if they had human capabilities is called *anthropomorphism* (from the Greek *anthropos,* meaning human being, and *morphe,* meaning form). Animals, of course, have neither human forms nor human minds, and we should not treat them as if they do. Nature is wonderful enough without trying to humanize it.

All nesting birds, of course, do not depend on injury feigning to defend their nests. The corncrake of the British Isles, a rail-like bird that lives in long grass, and also the American mockingbird will fight a rat or a cat until too crippled to escape. In either case, fighting or faking, the mother bird is likely to distract the attackers from the nest so that the young survive.

COLOR AND SHAPE

As with many other living organisms, protective coloration is a very important method of escape and survival for birds. Protective coloration is nature's camouflage. Ground-nesting birds depend upon it to a great extent. The striped plumage

Figure 8–5. Female least bittern at the nest. The least bittern depends on protective coloration to escape detection. Shape is also important. The least bittern contracts its feathers and points its bill straight up until it blends right in with the green reeds that surround it.

of the Wilson's snipe matches perfectly the grasses of open meadows and bogs. It needs only to crouch to achieve perfect concealment. The least bittern when disturbed draws its feathers so close to its body that it becomes as thin as the cattail reeds among which it hides. The disappearing act of the least bittern has earned it the nickname, "the genie of the bog." It depends on both color and shape for protection.

Once in a swamp I had cleared a path through some cattails to high ground near a nest I had found. I settled down with my field glasses to watch the bird returning to the nest. Presently a small, round-bodied, slim-headed, gawky looking bird appeared walking back to the nest. I recognized it as a least bittern. It could not be considered as really walking, for

Figure 8–6. Male least bittern. The least bittern is one of the best examples of protective coloration. It can draw its feathers so close to the body that it disappears among the slender cattail reeds. Although it is a common species, even in small swamps it is seldom observed.

it climbed along from stem to stem, keeping just above the surface of the water. The long, yellow flexible toes grasped the tangled reeds so efficiently that the bittern was able practically to run through the reeds.

When I stood up, the bird spotted me and contracted its feathers and pointed its long bill straight up. In this position it was almost impossible to distinguish. Like its larger relative, the American bittern, it depends on protective coloration and mimicry. Audubon showed that the least bittern could pass between two books set an inch apart without moving them, so great are its powers of constriction. The bird is a very poor flyer but seems to be specially designed for concealment.

Many species of birds freeze when they see the shadow of a hawk pass over. Hawks hunt principally by spotting movement and will pass over an immobile bird. Birds recognize hawks by their silhouettes.

One researcher cut out a cardboard wing pattern with a long, narrow extension in front and a short, broad extension in back. Turned one way, it looked like a long-necked, short-tailed goose; turned completely around, it resembled a short-necked, long-tailed Cooper's hawk. He fixed it to a wire and let it slide down the wire over the head of some quail. When the silhouette passed over with the long neck forward, like a goose, the quails ignored it. When it was reversed and passed over so that the short extension was forward and the long extension to the rear, like a hawk, the quail all froze in place and did not resume activity until the shadow had passed over. Movement and shape are important to both hawk and prey but perhaps most important to the prey. They provide concealment tactics and allow the camouflaged prey to live another day!

9. Bird Journeys: Migration and Dispersal

FROM EARLIEST TIMES PEOPLE HAVE SOUGHT AN EXPLANATION for the phenomenon of bird migration. They have hypothesized about the multitudes of whistling wings and gutteral calls which fill the skies on soft spring evenings. Persians and Arabs based parts of their calendar on dates taken from observations of the movement of birds. Many ancient peoples associated the return of birds with their spiritual festivals heralding the gods of spring. All sorts of folklore, myths, and legends surround the coming and going of birds.

Medieval peasants would indeed have been dull-witted not to notice that the birds of their fields varied from season to season. Even the most ignorant realized that bird movement depends on weather and the seasons. Some few, through superstition, concocted far-fetched theories to account for the disappearance of birds in the winter. One of these theories said that migrating swallows hibernated in mud banks. One of our current misconceptions is to think that the medievals were dull clods, all of whom believed that the world was flat.

Many medievals, however, had a good knowledge of bird

lore. Among them was Frederick II. Frederick corrected many of Aristotle's observations of birds, which were often based on hearsay or tradition and not on personal experience or experimentation as were Frederick's. Frederick was the father of migratory bird study. He knew where the swallows went in the winter, and he almost certainly knew the world was round from the work of an earlier scholar, Abu Abdullah Mohammed Idrisi.

Idrisi was an Arabian geographer attached to the court of Roger II, King of Sicily and Italy (1101–1154), at Palermo. In two manuscripts of his work *Al Rajori* (*The Going Out of a Curious Man to Explore the Regions of the Globe*) he recognizes that the earth is round. He also divides the known world into seven climates between the equator and the Arctic.

Frederick II was aware of the writings of Idrisi, for in the next century he seems to have followed the climatic divisions of Idrisi in his own work, *The Art of Falconry*. In his chapter 21, entitled "Of Early and Late Departure in Bird Migration, and of Their Flight Formation," he writes of ducks and geese that remain behind in the sixth and seventh climatic zones (arctic regions) because they can still find enough "herbage on which they feed."

Some of his other chapter titles are "Of Which Birds Migrate and at What Season," "Of the Reason Why Birds Migrate," "How Birds Prepare for Migration," and "Of the Seasons and Weather That Favor Migration." These chapters could be taken from a modern bird book. It might be well to acknowledge our debt to the brilliant thinkers of past centuries, for sometimes we make far too much of our modern accomplishments in science, which do, after all, stand on the shoulders of all ages. The interpretation of history is made more difficult by the egotism of each generation, which usually thinks it is much smarter than its predecessors.

WHY BIRDS MIGRATE

The reasons given by modern ornithologists for bird migration do not differ in any degree from those given by Frederick II. It is generally agreed that bird migration is a response to an unfavorable environment during a portion of the year in a particular region. Frederick sums it up very well in chapter 18 of *The Art of Falconry*:

> The reason why birds desert their usual resorts are numerous, but as we have said, it is chiefly to avoid excessively cold or very hot weather. For birds, like other living creatures, depend for their existence and survival upon a certain balance of fundamental conditions, and for this reason (since due proportion is conserved by moderate and destroyed by excessive heat or cold) birds require for their well being a moderation of the atmosphere and other environmental conditions, so they take refuge from extremes of either hot or cold.

Frederick then goes on to explain how cold and ice freeze the soil, making seeds, fruit, insects, and other foods very hard to obtain.

We have already pointed out that certain birds such as the tufted titmouse, the cardinal, and some woodpeckers are permanent residents and thus spend the entire year, winter included, on the Ozark plateau. If we look at a list of nonmigratory birds of the northern borders of the United States, we see essentially the same birds—cardinals, certain woodpeckers, and so forth. In other words, some birds fit the winter environment as well as the summer environment. Such birds are considered nonmigratory species because, although they disperse and wander about considerably, they remain at essentially the same latitudes as where they were reared. These birds have evolved to survive the rigors of winter, but they still must disperse in search of food.

Figure 9–1.   The male pine grosbeak is a bird of the great pine forests of Canada. It seldom disperses in the winter south of Kentucky. In December of 1968, I was treated to the rare sight of a flock of these rose-colored birds in my back yard in southern Georgia. My diary read as follows: "Tifton, Ga. 10:19 EST Dec. 21, 1968. Watching moon flight on TV when outside window saw first time grosbeaks as far south as Georgia. What kind of winter is this?"

For evolutionary reasons many biologists attribute the north-south movement of birds to environmental changes brought about by the beginning and the recession of the ice ages. However, since some birds are nonmigratory, some move north and south, some move east and west, and even a few

species, such as falcons, herons, and eagles, wander northward after the nesting season, no single theory explains why
birds migrate.

WHEN BIRDS MIGRATE

There is an excellent source for finding out about the migratory behavior of almost every American bird. It is Arthur
Cleveland Bent's famous book, *Life Histories of North American Birds,* which includes a paragraph or two about migration for each species. In many cases he gives the earliest and
latest arrival and departure dates in different regions.

His evaluation of the migratory habits of a species is based
on the recovery records of banded individuals. These records
kept in the files of the U.S. Fish and Wildlife Service are the
best indication of when and how far birds migrate. Records
show that some movement takes place during every month of
the year. In the summer, for instance, when the last robin has
started breeding in the north, the first shore birds are on their
way south. Most long-distance migratory flight, however, takes
place in spring and fall during, or following, the major
meteorological fluctuations of the changing seasons.

Dr. David Lack, Director of the Earl Grey Institute of Field
Ornithology at Oxford, in a paper entitled "The Influence of
Weather on Passerine Migration" concluded that warm spring
temperatures and cold fall temperatures are the weather factors that most influence migration. He believed that migration
is not influenced by the "general weather situation or by barometric pressure." He also did not consider air stability or
wind direction as a significant factor.

Although most students of bird migration would agree that
temperature is very important, certainly other climatic factors
contribute to the phenomenon. We have already talked about

Figure 9–2. The author holds a young peregrine falcon while a friend places a number band of the U.S. Fish and Wildlife Service on its leg. Banded birds are often recovered far from their nesting home, and such recovery records tell us much about their flight paths, direction, and time of migration.

the importance of day length (photoperiod) as a timing mechanism for migratory behavior. And anyone who has watched sea birds fly inland many hours before a hurricane along the coast of Florida must believe that birds can sense barometric pressure changes.

It has been demonstrated that spring migratory movement in the eastern United States begins when large tongues of warm, moist air push northward from the Gulf of Mexico.

Such warm fronts, as they are called, are associated with falling barometric pressures.

Dr. A. M. Bagg, a bird migration expert, and several colleagues postulated two types of migration "waves." One type they called the "onrushing wave," the other the "arrested wave." The onrushing wave takes place during the northern movement of low-pressure warm fronts, when southerly winds predominate. Birds move into and through the eastern United States with the passage of these warm fronts but preceding the

Figure 9–3.   Tree swallows line the telephone wires during fall and spring migration. The tree swallow breeds from northern Canada south to Arkansas and Virginia and winters from the United States Gulf Coast south to Cuba and Mexico. It nests in old woodpecker holes, crevices in buildings, or hollow trees. The tree swallow is the first swallow species to arrive in the North and the last to depart. They usually arrive in New York State on the heels of balmy spring temperatures in mid-April.

arrival of cold fronts. A cold front from the northwest, although followed by clear weather and a rising barometer, is preceded by cloudiness and rain as it approaches a northern-moving warm front. If a migratory wave of birds is moving northward when overtaken by the approaching cold front, then it is grounded where it is and forms an arrested wave. A bird watcher in Florida or along the Gulf Coast can utilize such knowledge to add to his bird list. Migrants that are not present during clear weather, because they are flying over, suddenly appear with the arrival of bad weather because they are grounded. The most comfortable weather may not be the best weather for bird watching.

HOW FAR BIRDS FLY

The champion long-distance flier, and the one most noted in literature, is the arctic tern. Its summer and winter homes are 11,000 miles apart. The tern flies in a roundabout route from its breeding ground in arctic North America and Greenland, across the Atlantic, and then down the coast of Europe and Africa to the antarctic. Some terns fly back across the Atlantic and, instead of following the coast of Africa, follow the coast of South America to the antarctic.

Birds store large amounts of fat for these long flights, but the water and nonfat tissue remains stable despite the build-up of huge fat reserves before migration. This is not true of humans. In humans tissue and water are added to the body as well as fat, and this makes reducing a slow process. The migratory bird, however, easily burns up this extra fat, utilizing it as "high octane" fuel, like an airplane with extra wing tanks.

Size has little to do with the distance migratory birds fly. The tiny blackpoll warbler is believed to fly from its nesting grounds in New England, directly south across the Atlantic Ocean to the West Indies, and then on to South America as far as Chile. This is a tremendous overwater flight for a bird weighing only eleven to twenty grams. The bobolink, which breeds in the northern United States and is larger than the blackpoll, follows the eastern coast of the United States to the West Indies and then flies on to its winter grounds in middle South America. It does not cut across the Atlantic Ocean to the West Indies as the much smaller blackpoll does.

The fall migratory route of the New England blackpoll warbler may involve the longest nonstop flight over water of any small passerine bird. The blackpoll returns by way of Florida. Some return to New England, and the rest scatter across the width of the United States. The westernmost blackpolls arrive in Alaska by May 30, and the eastern birds arrive in New England by May 20. Birds such as the blackpoll that begin migration late in the spring advance with longer and longer flights as they move from south to north with the season. In the southern regions the migratory flights may only cover 30 to 40 miles a day but increase with the northward movement to 200 or more miles per day.

Birds that are partially migratory move across only a few states. The common blue jay, for instance, may move south from Massachusetts to North Carolina in the eastern United States, or from Wisconsin to Arkansas in the West.

LONG-RANGE DISPERSAL

Dispersal is a bird movement phenomenon confused with migration. Dispersal differs from migration as the direct flow of a river following its bed differs from flood waters sweeping across an area. Again it seems to be Frederick II who first distinguished dispersal from migration. He pointed out that herons disperse from their nesting sites over large areas, spreading out fan-wise. Some even move north after the breeding season.

True migratory birds follow definite flyways. There are four main flyways across the United States: the Atlantic (east of the Appalachian mountains), the Missisippi, the Central, and the Pacific. The width of these aerial highways varies

Figure 9–4.   Great blue heron at the nest. Young herons, when they leave the nest, disperse from their nesting sites over large areas. Such movement is considered long-range dispersal and not true migration.

considerably with species. The path of some migratory birds may spread out over hundreds of miles while others are confined to narrow routes only a few miles wide.

Dr. Joseph Hickey, professor of ornithology at the University of Wisconsin, divides dispersal movements into three types—periodic, annual, and irregular or accidental. Periodic dispersal is an extension of range that occurs at various time intervals among the species. Such extensions are usually caused by some ecological change. An example is the shortage of the small northern rodents called lemmings which occurs periodically in the arctic. The shortage causes the snowy owl to disperse far south of its normal range in search of food. Audubon has reported seeing the snowy owl as far south as Arkansas. A flight of the snowy owls in 1945 was estimated to contain 14,409 sighted individuals within the borders of the United States.

Annual dispersal occurs in species, such as herons and certain birds of prey, which disperse after the young are fledged. Irregular dispersal occurs when birds are caught up by high winds or freak gales and are driven on long, sustained flights to new regions. The English ornithologist H. F. Witherby writes an account of a crested plover which was driven in twenty-four hours from England to the coast of Newfoundland. The African cattle egret, which is now established as a resident bird in the southern United States, is thought to have reached the West Indies and the United States in this manner. Hickey's three types of dispersal might be best qualified with the adjective "temporary," because the cattle egret, although it arrived at our shores as an accidental or irregular traveler, nevertheless acquired an ecological foothold in the United States. It has become a permanent resident. This type of permanent dispersal, by which a bird expands its range into new ecologically suitable regions, is called "spread."

The starling is another example of spread. This bird was first introduced by Mr. Eugene Schiefflin in 1890, when he released sixty birds in Central Park in New York City. The starling was first reported in Wisconsin on February 17, 1923, by Herbert L. Stoddard. By 1935 it had spread to northern Wisconsin. Banding records indicate that a starling's range is localized to an area of approximately thirty-five miles, yet in fifty years starlings have spread across half of our continent.

HOW BIRDS FLY

The primary and secondary feathers of a bird's wing have different aerodynamic functions. Like an airplane, the bird wing has a broad leading edge. The secondary feathers are attached to the wing parallel to the bird's body. They represent the airfoil, or lift portion of the wing. The force that opposes the weight of the bird is called *lift*, and the resistance of the air to the forward movement of the bird is called *drag*. Lift is generated by the flow of air across the wing above and below the secondaries. Since the leading edge of the wing is broad and the top surface curved upward, air striking the wing has to travel further over the curved top than across the bottom. The result is that air velocity across the top increases. This increase in velocity creates a drop in pressure (a partial vacuum) above the wing. The air beneath the wing is moving relatively more slowly because of the shorter distance it travels. This produces a corresponding increase in pressure beneath the wing. The greater pressure below pushes the wing, and the bird, upward into the partial vacuum.

In order to overcome drag, the bird has to move forward fast enough for the air flow to generate lift. The primaries serve this function as they are arranged to strike the air at right angles to the bird's body and serve as the propeller of

Figure 9–5. A small group of Canadian geese breed on Payne's Prairie in central Florida. Most Canadian geese, however, spend the winter in the South but breed in northern Canada. Migrating geese that winter in Florida begin their northern journey on the first full moon in March. Flying wedges of Canadian geese are the harbingers of spring, and their babbling honks fill the sky along their northern flyways.

the bird. The primaries pull the bird forward on the down stroke. The same lift principle is involved; as the primary feathers are forced forward and downward, the broad leading edge of each primary acts as a small airfoil. There is more pressure behind the feather than in front, and so each feather pulls the bird ahead as it is forced into its own partial vacuum. Bird feathers are flexible and automatically change pitch (twist) according to their position during their flight. On the backward upstroke, they twist and push back against the air, which also draws the bird forward. Thus the forward motion that overcomes drag is generated both on the up and the down strokes.

WHY BIRDS MIGRATE IN FORMATION

Aerodynamicists have suspected that long-distance migratory birds adapt the V formation in order to reduce the amount of energy needed for such long flights.* It has been shown that formation flight improves aerodynamic efficiency. According to theoretical calculations twenty-five birds flying in V formation can fly some 70 percent farther than a lone bird. The advantage is even greater when there is a tail wind. The extreme range of formation flight depends on the vertical wash behind each wing. Beyond a forward-moving wing tip there is an upwash which is very strong. The strong upwash beyond the tip creates a favorable forward interference for other birds flying abreast in side-by-side formation. Each bird flies in the upwash of its companion. The effect is similar to flying in a thermal upcurrent, where less total lift power is needed. When the tip spacing between flying birds is small, the drag is also reduced. Birds flying in formation adjust their forward speed so that each bird flies at its maximum lift to drag ratio.

This explanation applies to line-abreast flight. However, only the birds in the center have the maximum drag savings because they are flying in the upwash field of birds on both sides. In the V formation the center bird flies in a weaker upwash on both sides from the birds flying behind.

The rear birds are in a favorable upwash on only one side from the birds directly ahead of them. However, they are in a much more strongly developed total upwash field from all of

*For an explanation of insect and bird aerodynamics, see *Insect Behavior* by the author.

the forward birds. Thus we see that in the V formation the drag savings are evenly distributed among all of the birds. How marvelous that close cooperation between birds should not only increase their flight range by 70 percent, but also provide us with that breath-taking symbol of the seasons— long Vs of geese winging across the skies.

Figure 9–6. White ibis against the rising moon. Dr. George Lowery of Louisiana State University developed a system of studying nocturnal migration by observing night-flying birds against the full moon. A telescope is pointed at the moon and the ground observer counts the silhouettes of birds crossing the face of the moon. Using this method Dr. Lowery and a colleague, Dr. Newman, found that herons, geese, and shore birds migrate in close formation but that small song birds fly alone at night. They also found that nocturnal migrants fly with the wind and that the number of migrating birds drop off after midnight.

10. Bird Communication: Song and Display

BIRDS COMMUNICATE WITH EACH OTHER BY SOUND AND VISION. Both of these senses are well-developed in all birds, but the senses of smell and taste are not believed to be well-developed. In this characteristic birds differ considerably from insects and mammals, both of which have well-developed senses of chemoreception.* Insects detect food and chemical sex attractants (called pheromones) with their antennae. Many animals use their noses to locate both food and mates.

A bird has very few taste buds on its tongue. Practically nothing is known about taste with regard to the behavior of food selection in birds. Darwin believed that birds cannot smell; however, in the Cathartidae (New World vulture) the olfactory (smell) chamber is well-developed. Experiments have shown that the turkey vulture is able to locate food by smell. Such is not the case for our common black vulture.

*"Chemoreception" is a term loosely applied to the senses of smell and taste since both involve the biological detection of chemical molecules.

Much more physiological and behavioral research is needed before any definite conclusions can be reached regarding the senses of smell or taste in birds.

THE SYRINX AND EAR

Birds have a special voice box called the *syrinx*. In mammals the voice box is called the *larynx* and is located at the head of the windpipe (trachea). The bird syrinx is at the lower end of the trachea where it branches into the two *bronchial tubes* that lead to the lungs.

The ear, as pointed out in Chapter 2, is located on the side of the head hidden under the *auricular patch*—a patch of feathers that covers the ear opening. There is no external ear flap, or outer ear, as in mammals. The *external auditory* canal opens directly on the side of the head (Chapter 2, Fig. 2–10). As in mammals there is a *tympanic membrane* (eardrum) located at the end of the auditory canal.

The owl, which hunts at night and can catch its prey in total darkness, has specialized ears for homing in on that prey. The ears are asymmetrical—of different size and shape on each side. Furthermore, the openings of the external auditory canal are not on the same level on each side of the head. This arrangement allows the owl to pinpoint the prey by special signal processing of the low-intensity sounds made by the prey as it moves.

THE VOICES OF SPRING

Song is one of the most important means of communication in birds. What we hear as the delightful melodies of spring are for birds an intricate mechanism of species survival. In most species it is the male bird that is the singer. Bird songs

Figure 10–1. Male cardinal giving its territorial or advertising song. Birds often choose special perches within the territory to sing from. This cardinal had a special song perch in the author's back yard in Gainesville, Florida. The cardinal is one of the species in which the female's territorial song is almost as elaborate as that of the male.

and calls are communication signals that insure reproduction and egg laying in the species.

Ornithologists have classified bird song into three main categories:

1. *Territorial songs,* which repel other birds of the same sex while attracting a mate.
2. *Signal songs,* which coordinate the behavioral activities of courting or mated and nesting birds.
3. *Female songs,* which occur in some species of birds; for instance, both the male and the female mockingbird sing.

The word "song" as used in the literature of bird study is a generalized term. Some ornithologists have suggested that the term "song" be restricted to only those vocal patterns of *territory-owning* males. Niko Tinbergen, the famous English animal behaviorist, calls such vocal patterns "advertising song." He states that the male is advertising for a mate while at the same time advertising to repel any male competitor.

M. Moynihan of the Smithsonian Institution in his analysis of tropical American song birds points out that such a definition may be too narrow. He defines a song as "any vocal pattern which, when uttered by one bird, usually repels other birds of the same sex and of the same species and attracts other birds of the opposite sex." By this definition a song may be any sound or series of notes, from the complex melody of the mockingbird (whether it owns a territory or not) to the very simple "loose quavering trill," all in the same pitch, of the Oregon junco.

The tropical brown-capped bush tanager utters an extremely hard, short vocalization called a rattle. Dr. Moynihan describes the rattle as a rapid series of very short "tuck" notes. This rattle is associated only with the hostile display of the bush tanagers. Since it is given separately from the series of sounds that the bird uses to attract a mate, it is not a bird song in the sense of the definition accepted by ornithologists.

The sexual attraction calls of this species are made up of sounds that Dr. Moynihan describes as "flourishes," dawn-calling performances, plaintive notes, and muffled rattles. He states that the bush tanagers do not have any single vocal pattern in their repertory that could be classified as a song in the true sense. However, if the bird utters a rattle together with what he calls a flourish, the two calls together may produce the same effect as the true songs of other species. Together they are a "song," but given separately the two calls have the

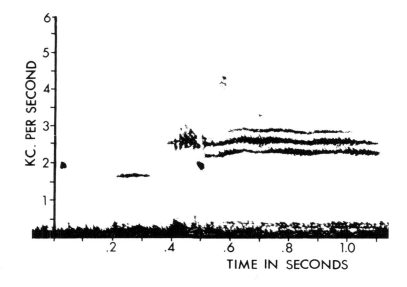

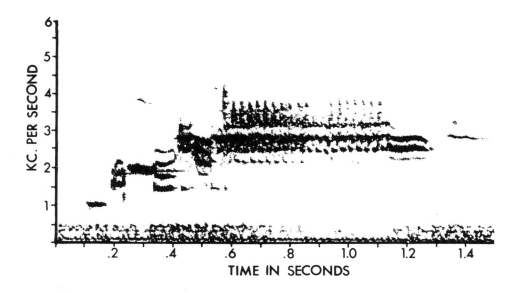

Figure 10–2. Audiospectrograms of song of two different races of red-winged blackbird (gubernator, top, and nelsoni, bottom) showing differences in physical structure of the songs that can be discerned by the ear but are difficult to describe in words. These two races cohabited the Lerma Marshes west of Mexico City and were not interbreeding (after Hardy and Dickerman, 1965).
LIVING BIRD, CORNELL UNIVERSITY ANNUAL.

separate functions of territorial defense and mate finding, so the definition does not fit.

If we accept the above definition (and we must define behavior patterns if we are to understand them), then we see that "songs" may range from one-syllable notes or harsh calls to the beautiful vocalizations of our southern mockingbird, but they must always be associated with hostile display (either in setting up or in defending a territory) and mate finding together.

Figure 10–3.   Are sound signals learned or inherited? The gaping response of nestlings is a visible display signal accompanied by sound, usually a querulous cheeping. This display signal is inherited. These nestling lark sparrows gape and cheep even at night (when this flash picture was taken) if the shadow of a large object passes over them. The mother bird responds to this signal display by stuffing the gaping mouths with food.

The question of how birds "learn" their songs has intrigued bird behaviorists from earliest times. Modern sound-recording techniques have been utilized to sort out and correlate bird songs with the observed physical behavior of certain species. The songs are recorded and then converted from a tape to a visual graph called an *audiospectrograph*.

The audiospectrograph is a series of lines, bars, slashes, or dashes that represent the audio components of the song. Songs of different species, or individuals of a species, can be closely analyzed by comparing the frequencies and shapes of the slashes and bars on the graph.

Peter Marler and his colleagues at the University of California studied song development in hand-raised Oregon juncos. They raised eight male juncos in acoustic isolation from each other and from wild juncos. Each bird developed several characteristic song types. The songs of the birds that were raised in isolation were somewhat longer, with fewer and longer syllables, than those of wild birds. Their songs were also more variable. Each of the experimental birds had at least one "wild type" song. The experimental birds that were raised in a "rich auditory environment" (surrounded by recorded songs of many other species of birds) developed more song types and a much more elaborate syllable structure. The researchers concluded that these more complex songs were not learned by pure imitation but developed from some "unspecific audio stimulation" that caused the birds to improvise new songs. In other words, vocal inventiveness is a characteristic of bird song development in many species.

In another similar study Peter Goldman of Ohio State University played songs of field sparrows that were strangers, field sparrows from neighboring territories, synthetic (made-up songs), and songs of two other species to male field sparrows. He discovered that the males did not respond to the songs of other species, but they did respond to a synthetic song that resembled in tempo the song of a real field sparrow. They did not respond to the song of a neighboring bird when the song of the neighbor was played near the common territorial border of the two males. They did respond with an answering song to the song of a strange bird played near the boundary of the territory. If the strange bird song was played within the territorial borders of the male owner, the owner responded with flight. Thus we see that field sparrows react to strange males (1) by singing to advertise their presence to females in competition with the stranger or (2) by flight if the strange bird intrudes into the territory. Flight readies the territorial owner for the threat of the intruder.

These recording experiments indicate that the male birds learn and also improvise songs by listening to adults of their own species. However, some of the singing ability is also innate. All of the Oregon juncos, for instance, had at least one wild type song even though raised in isolation. It is quite evident that birds can distinguish the songs of territorial neighbors from those of strange birds that have not set up a territory near by.

SIGNAL SONGS

Signal songs are usually more in evidence during the nesting period. They coordinate and synchronize the feeding and nesting activities of mated pairs. They are also utilized to synchronize and coordinate courtship behavior. They may resemble the territorial song or be much shorter and simpler.

Some species of birds share incubation. They must change on the nest with as little clumsiness as possible so as to avoid damaging the eggs. When a male nightjar (which nests on the bare ground) approaches the incubating female, he mutters a curious "quaw-ee, quaw-ee" note. The female responds with soft churrs. They snuggle up close together, churring and swaying their bodies, until suddenly the female flies off leaving her mate on the eggs. The "quaw-ees" and simple churring notes are signal songs. They coordinate the risky changeover on the nest.

DISPLAY BEHAVIOR

If electronic recording equipment is essential to the study of bird songs, then sharp eyes and detailed observations are essential for studying bird display. To make any sense at all of the many peculiar activities of a species, it may be necessary to devote weeks and months to watching and recording the overall activity of a bird in the field.

Really to understand each specific detail of display behavior, one must get a broad picture, perhaps we should call it an outline map, of the behavior of the species. All display behavior must fit and relate to the overall behavior of the species. Like a road sign on a map in relation to the other roads, a display signal must have a relationship to all other display signals given by a bird species. A concise description of an isolated bird display incident will not point the right direction to travel in such a study if the overall map of behavior is unknown.

In the chapter on reproduction we defined display behavior and pointed out that it is associated with the following: (1) defense of the territory, or *threat display*, (2) courtship, or *epigamic display*, and (3) maintaining the pair-bond, or *postnuptial display*. Many ornithologists include another type that they call *distraction display*. Injury feigning described in the chapter on defense is an example of distraction display. Since most of these types of display have been covered else-

Figure 10–4. The magpie lark of Australia is neither a magpie nor a lark. The author noticed this one flashing the startling white tail and wing patches in the park in Sidney, Australia. The jerky gait and excited "pee-o-wit" call of the bird was very threatening and demonstrated a determined sense of territory. The name "magpie lark" probably came from the fact that the bird is shaped like a lark and has a black bib and back like a magpie.

where in the book, we will discuss the most complex display behavior, courtship display, in this chapter.

COURTSHIP DISPLAY

Along with song, movements and posturing of a specialized type are a part of social communication in birds. Body movements and stylized postures are a visual language and convey specific information from the displaying bird to the observing bird. In many cases the movements are very complex and may be stylized to a degree that they are actually ritualized into special "dances." The color of the bird (usually but not always the male) may enter into the special meaning of a display posture or dance. Whenever colored parts of the bird are utilized in display behavior, they are always positioned so as to be clearly visible, such as the fluffing of the robin's red breast or the raising of a brightly colored crest. Some birds have special colorful feathers or organs that have evolved for special display behavior. The beautiful plumage of the birds of paradise is the best example of special display plumage.

Display behavior synchronizes the activities of the sexes. Behaviorists refer to the displaying bird as the *actor* and the observing bird as the *reactor*. The bird that initates the display (the actor) is usually the male, the female being the reactor. There are exceptions, however, and in some species the female may be the actor and initiate the display behavior.

Behavior which usually begins as threat behavior on the part of the actor bird defending its territory may change to acceptance if an appropriate display countersignal is given by a reactor bird. A display signal that suppresses aggressiveness on the part of the actor or escape on the part of the reacting bird is called *appeasement* display. Typical bird display patterns follow a sequence of events from aggression, through

Figure 10–5. The Florida gallinule is called the water hen in the South. It does resemble a chicken, and the two solid black young resemble little chicks. On the underside of the outer tail feathers are two conspicuous white flags. They may serve as display signals in the courtship of the bird. The tail coverts flash with each quick upward jerk of the tail. It is also an excellent visible signal for the small chicks that might lose sight of the mother in the thick marshes where the gallinules breed.

appeasement display, to courtship display, mating, and finally postnuptial display and nesting. This is what is meant by a sequence of display patterns in the life history of a species.

The courtship display of the white-rumped sandpiper has been described in detail by William H. Drury. It is a good example of a display sequence, for it is intricate and includes both ground and aerial display. It begins when the male approaches another bird in an aggressive posture—head thrust forward, back feathers ruffled, wings spread, tail slightly cocked, and the body in a crouching run. Appeasement takes place if the female stands her ground with the head and neck stretched upward. The male then stops and stands with his neck and head in a similar position. The "head held high" posture is the flee-appeasement display of many plovers and sandpipers.

The white-rumped sandpiper performs a courtship dance

with the wings stiffly spread, tail cocked straight up, and head thrust forward, all the while calling "bzzzzip." There is also an aerial display flight in which the bird flies up in the air fifty to seventy-five feet where it hovers or sails, emitting a trill-like call which ends in a "zip-zip" tone as it floats to the ground.

There are, of course, variations in the display repertoire of the sandpiper. Although the courtship display of most birds is quite stylized and is inherited behavior, there are, nevertheless, variations of the generalized form. As with song there may be more than one rendering of the basic form.

THE BIRD DANCE

Courtship display may range all the way from very simple movements, such as the quivering drooped wings of the female house sparrow as she solicits copulation with the male, to the courtship dances of cranes and emus.

Cranes are among the best-known of bird dancers. On Payne's Prairie near Gainesville, Florida, where I live, I have watched the stately sandhill crane perform an interesting dance. It usually takes place on the breeding ground but is also performed in almost every month of the year. Because it is not confined to the breeding period alone, most bird behaviorists believe the dance is a "get acquainted" affair. Two tall graceful birds face each other and stalk about bowing and capering before each other. Every once in awhile with wings half spread, they leap five or six feet into the air.

Some birds, such as the American prairie chicken, have special breeding grounds called dance arenas. Here the males meet and perform their complex display dances. Such birds do not form a pair-bond, and the arena dance serves to synchronize the male and female reproductive rhythms.

People have always been intrigued by the courtship dances of birds and often imitate them in their own ritual dances. The American Indians copied the dance of the prairie chicken. The Chuckhee people of Siberia imitate the notes and posturing of the dance of a sandpiper-like bird called the ruff.

An ancient dance called the crane dance is said to have been performed by Theseus on his return from Crete with the youths and maidens saved from the Minotaur. The "dance of the white crane" was also performed in China around 500 B.C. Neither East nor West has held a monopoly on copying the display dances of birds.

THE RELEASER

The animal behaviorist Niko Tinbergen has labeled the display signals of birds and other animals *releasers*. Tinbergen states that although the sex drive is the main motivating force in animals, aggressiveness and escape are also very important factors. Aggressiveness and escape behavior contradict one another. However, Dr. Tinbergen believes that in each animal there is a good balance between all of these behavioral drives. Song and display are the audio and visual communication signals that lead the bird from the antisocial aggressive or escape drives to the social drive of reproduction. After all, if there were no signals to overcome the aggressive territorial drives of the male or the escape drives of the intruding birds, there could be no social interaction between individuals, and mating would never occur.

It is for this reason that Dr. Tinbergen prefers the term releaser for such display signals. A releaser is any stimulus (display signal or song) that serves to initiate reflex behavior in another organism. In other words, each species of bird has inherent within its biological makeup certain patterns of behavior which depend upon special sound or visual signals for release. Within the behavioral pattern of each species, a releaser signal must precede each action in the chain of events leading to the mating. If a bird is expecting a releaser signal and for some reason it does not come, then the next behavioral reaction, which is dependent on the signal for release, cannot take place.

Many behaviorists believe that if an animal or bird is waiting for a releaser signal from its partner and the signal is not

Figure 10–6.   A "jack" snipe in courtship flight. The long unique bill is used to probe the soft mud of bogs and tundra for insect larvae. During the mating season the male produces a spiritlike winnowing sound that haunts the late evening sky. It is a courtship call produced by the vibrating outer tail feathers during the downward plunge of the display flight.

given, then the animal is left with a strongly aroused but thwarted sex drive. This leaves the animal in a state of tension, and a form of behavior called *displacement activity* occurs.

Displacement activity is a substitute "tension relieving" activity. It takes the place of, or displaces, the normal response that would have followed had the expected releaser signal been forthcoming. Some behaviorists term such activities "false activities" because they fall outside the usual behavioral repertoire of the bird. They are a side-tracking of the built-up energy in the bird.

Displacement activity may include such behavior as displacement feeding, bathing, false nest building, and preening. Much of the preening observed in nature is displacement preening. Razorbills, for instance, break off fighting in order to false preen. Puck, my Australian cockatoo, false preens to the extent that he pulls out his feathers and is partially naked. Presumably the cockatoo's sex drive is thwarted because it has no mate.

There are no other areas of bird life that are as fascinating and intriguing as that of display behavior. The student of display behavior must be a master detective dedicated to solving some of the fundamental mysteries of life.

11. Fun with Birds

BIRDS, LIKE ALL LIVING ORGANISMS, HAVE BEEN GIVEN SCI-
entific names derived from Latin or Greek. Fortunately, to
identify birds in the field one does not need to know scientific
names. Strangely enough, the English names of birds are
seldom changed, while taxonomists often change the scientific
name of an organism for reasons pertaining to the classification of the plant or animal.

HOW TO IDENTIFY BIRDS

The best way to identify a bird is with the help of one of
the good field guides. Two are especially recommended:
Peterson's *A Field Guide to the Birds* (Boston: Houghton
Mifflin Co.) and *Guide to Field Identification: Birds of North
America* by Robbins, Bruun, Zim, and Singer (New York:
Golden Press). I prefer the latter, which is a paperback, has
excellent color illustrations, and also has distribution maps.
Distribution maps are very important, for they tell one

whether or not a bird appears in certain areas. A flicker might be sighted, for instance, when the observer cannot see the underside of the wings well enough to tell if it is a yellow-shafted or a red-shafted flicker. A distribution map will show that the red-shafted flicker occurs only in the West and the yellow-shafted flicker in the East. We would not expect to see a red-shafted flicker in Florida or New York; however, their range overlaps in the Midwest, so a Texas bird watcher would be on the lookout for both species.

Certain birds are given local or regional names which, however descriptive, confuse the novice bird watcher. For instance, in the South the Cooper's hawk is called the big blue darter. The latter name is much more descriptive than Cooper's hawk. Field guides utilize only the common names approved by the American Ornithologists Union. Those are the names to learn in order to avoid confusion.

Most bird watchers prefer to identify birds by sight, but songs are also an excellent aid to identification. *Birds of North America* contains a section on interpreting song audiospectrographs. The book uses the system developed by Dr. Peter Kellogg at Cornell University. Audiospectrographs of the songs of many common birds are presented along with the distribution maps.

An even easier way to learn the more common bird songs and calls is to listen to them on phonograph records or cassette tapes. The Cornell University Laboratory of Ornithology produced a series called the "Peterson's Field Guide Records." They include the songs of both eastern and western birds. They also produced birdsong cassettes. Dover Records produces an excellent record called "Bird Song and Bird Behavior." This record is of particular interest to the student interested in the relationship of song to bird behavior.

Most birds can be identified by sight, but it is not always

as easy as the books intimate. Birds can be illusive creatures, and the dappled light and dark of deep woodlands play tricks on the eyes. A good pair of binoculars is a necessity.

The Binocular

In order to choose a good binocular the serious bird watcher should know something about how they work. After all, the idea is to see the bird clearly in order to identify it and observe its behavior. There are three characteristics of binoculars that should be kept in mind when purchasing a pair— magnification, field of view, and light transmission.

Magnification and light transmission qualities are usually marked on the binoculars. Stamped beside the eye pieces are the figures 6x25, 7x35, 7x50, 10x50, or some combination of numbers. The first number represents the power of magnification (6 times, and so forth), and the second number represents the diameter of the objective (front lens) in millimeters (35, 50, and so forth). The latter is a measurement of the light transmission characteristic of the binocular. The larger the diameter, the greater the light transmission through the lens to the eye.

A glass that magnifies seven times makes a bird seventy feet away appear to be only ten feet from the observer. To determine the brightness or light transmitting power of the glass, divide the diameter of the objective by the magnification and square the results:

$$\frac{35\text{mm}}{7\text{x}} = 5\text{x}5 = 25 \text{ for a 7x35 glass}$$

$$\frac{50\text{mm}}{7\text{x}} = 7.14\text{x}7.14 = 50 \text{ for a 7x50 glass}$$

Thus we see that a fifty-millimeter seven-power glass has twice the light transmission capability of a thirty-five-millimeter seven-power glass.

For most purposes the 7x35 glass is the best compromise. Glasses with 50-millimeter objectives, although they have excellent light transmission, are rather bulky to carry about. Too much magnification can also be a handicap under certain conditions, for unsteady movements by the arms and hands are magnified just like the bird. High-power binoculars are very difficult to hold still enough so that the bird does not appear to vibrate and blur. This can cause severe eyestrain and is very frustrating. Seven-power glasses usually have a field of view of 420 feet at 1,000 yards (it may be less or more depending on the make). This means that the viewing field of objects 1,000 yards away is 420 feet across (from side to side). The wider the field of view, the easier it is quickly to pick out and spot a moving bird. Medium power, wide-field binoculars allow one to swing the glasses quickly onto the bird with enough steadiness to pick up all the detail of plumage.

Since the field of view depends on magnification, ten-power glasses usually do not have a field of view of more than 350 to 370 feet at 1,000 yards. However, there are special design wide-field, high-power glasses.

The lower light transmission power of thirty-five-millimeter glasses is more than compensated for in modern binoculars by hard-coating. The lenses are treated with an antireflection coating which reduces the reflection of light from the glass surfaces. Coating doubles the brightness so that the light transmission of twenty-five of 7x35 binoculars becomes fifty with coated lenses (equal to an uncoated 7x50 glass). The lenses of coated binoculars have a bluish color to them. Demand coated lenses when purchasing new binoculars.

Another important consideration is that your binoculars have a center focus knob. It is almost impossible to adjust two eye pieces separately while tracking a fast-moving bird flitting through the branches. Most good center-focus binoculars also have a right eye adjustment so that the two eyepieces can be adjusted for differences of vision between the two eyes.

In the field it is always an advantage to wear an eye shade or visored cap. Open sunlight causes the pupils to contract so that most of the light from the binoculars falls on the outer iris of the eye. When the eyes are shaded, the pupils expand, and all the light from the binoculars is utilized by the sensitive pupils.

Recognizing Form

Beginning bird watchers often make the mistake of depending on color alone for identification. In separating a bird into a group or family, however, shape and form are more important than color. For instance, chickadees, creepers, wrens, and nuthatches are all found around the trunks of trees feeding on small insects. Each has a quite different silhouette, however, and once the form or silhouette of a bird is imprinted on the mind, it will never be forgotten. Experienced bird watchers can tell certain bird forms at a glance, even from the sides of the eyes. One caution, however—it is almost impossible to identify some birds without actually observing their minute field markings. Peterson's *Field Guide to the Birds* is particularly good for pointing out the distinctive markings of close look-alike birds. When in doubt, refer to this excellent book!

LIFE HISTORY OF A SPECIES

A life history is a study of a single species of bird. In most bird books the life histories of even the well-known species cover only one or two pages for each species. As pointed out in Chapter 7, amateurs such as Henry Elliot Howard, who was a businessman, have contributed some of the most significant research findings to our knowledge of bird life. Arthur

Cleveland Bent, who wrote the famous *Life Histories of North American Birds* was a Massachusetts businessman.

Amateurs sometimes have an advantage over professionals. For one thing, there is no pressure for the amateur to finish his work and rush it into print. He may take a lifetime to study the behavior and life history of one species. For another thing, the really observant amateur may bring a fresh approach to his study. Scientists, like everyone else, can get in a rut with outdated or textbook answers that may not be true at all or, at least, may furnish only a partially valid answer to some research problem.

The two prerequisites for a life history study are first, the ability to observe accurately, and second, the self-discipline to record detailed observations in a field notebook. The truly accurate observer never depends on memory but records immediately in his notebook even the most minor events. Details that may of themselves seem insignificant often lead to important findings.

It is suggested that before starting a life history study the reader examine some of the life histories in one of Arthur Cleveland Bent's volumes, because Mr. Bent has brought together much of the literature on each species of bird. He follows an outline that covers these factors: habits, nesting, eggs, incubating, plumage, food, behavior, voice, field marks, distribution, migration, and egg dates.

Since a life history is a continuing project, only certain aspects can be covered during any one season. An outline for a life history study is an aid in deciding what aspects of the life history to concentrate on. It will enable the observer to program his time to fit the species. Obviously, life history studies for the amateur are usually restricted to common species that can be observed close to home. The golden eagle would not be a logical subject for the average high school student. Interestingly enough, little is known about some of our most common garden and woodland songbirds.

Suggested Outline for a Life History Study

1. Taxonomy of the species
   a. Search of the literature for the description of the species.
   b. Who first described it?
   c. Relation of the species to other birds.
   d. Fossil records.

2. Distribution
   a. Occurrence of the species in your state, in the United States, similar species or related races in other areas of the world.
   b. Summer and winter range.

3. Habitat
   a. Feeding and nesting.
   b. Type of cover utilized.
   c. Roosting or flocking areas.

4. Food and feeding habits
   a. Adult food habits.
   b. What kind of food is taken to the nest? How often? What kind of insects are eaten?
   c. Do food habits vary with the season?

5. Territory
   a. Do males defend a territory?
   b. How large? Do the boundaries overlap with those of other species or shift?
   c. What are the roosting and feeding territories?

6. Courtship
   a. Formation of the pair-bond.

      b. Display behavior.
      c. Song.
      d. Copulation.

7. Nesting
    a. Size of nest, construction technique, material, eggs, clutch size, date eggs laid, sex performing incubation, dates of hatching, weight and size of nestlings, changes in plumage, dates of nest leaving, foraging for young.
    b. Behavior and development of young.

8. Song
    a. Type of song.
    b. Does the female sing?
    c. Song perches.

9. Migration
    a. Dates of arrival and departure.
    b. Peak of migration.
    c. Effect of weather on migration.

10. General
    a. Longevity
    b. Association with other birds, mammals, invertebrates.
    c. Relationships to humans, beneficial effects for humans, damage to humans' interests.
    d. Folklore, local or regional names.

Of course, the above outline would not suffice for all birds, nor is it by any means complete. Keep in mind that conclusions should not be based on only a few observations. Accuracy depends on as many observations as are possible under field conditions.

COVER MAPPING AND POPULATION STUDIES

To understand the bird life of an area, it is necessary to know not only which species are present, but also the relative abundance of each species. Other important factors in a population study should include observation of which species breed in the area and which do not, the distribution and dens-

Figure 11–1.   Cover mapping an area. Each type habitat is paced off by foot. The area of the different habitats can be checked by making a grid on a piece of transparent plastic. The size of each grid square is checked by laying it over a known U.S. topographical map. Since the area of each grid square is known it can be placed over your own drawing to check the accuracy of your map sketch based on the paced-off measurements.

ity of individuals and species in relation to the habitat preference, arrival and departure dates of migratory birds, and
a host of other particulars.

Studies such as these require intensive observation over a
limited area. The basic technique of such a study consists of
frequent (at least once a week) bird censuses of the study
area.

The majority of field records in a population study will be
sight records. Calls should be utilized if the observer is absolutely acquainted with the distinctive song of the species.
Ornithologists say that a common bird with a familiar call has
a high percentage of conspicuousness: that is, it is easily recognized by sight or call and is recorded often. Such a bird
would be the common crow. Some birds that are inconspicuous to sight, such as a wood thrush or ovenbird, nevertheless
are very distinctive because of their easily recognized calls.

Birds that are conspicuous and are easily recorded by sight
or sound introduce a certain amount of error into any population study. They are obviously recorded more often and with
less search effort than rare or inconspicuous birds. A bird
such as a sharp-shinned hawk might occur in a woodlot yet
never be seen because of its secretive habits.

For each observation, the sex, where possible, and the im-
mediate habitat of the bird should be recorded in the field
book. In the eastern United States, with the exception of the
Deep South, habitats might be broken down into cover areas
similar to those shown by the author for the Lake Wedington
study. Many regions, such as the western mountains and
deserts, contain unique habitats. The plant life in such areas
may require a more specialized terminology.

Field guides to the trees and shrubs of the region under
study should be consulted. *A Field Guide to Trees and Shrubs*
by George A. Petrides, which is in the Peterson field guide

series, is a good example. Local libraries may be able to recommend books that cover the common trees, shrubs, and weeds of your region. One of the best guides for identifying weeds is *Weeds of the North Central States* (circular 718), which can be obtained free from the Agricultural Experiment Station of the University of Illinois. The agricultural experiment station of almost every state university publishes circulars and bulletins that cover the state's plant life. They are given away or sold at very nominal fees on request to the extension service of the state agricultural experiment station. With the help of such guides the novice researcher should be able to identify the trees, shrubs, grasses, and weeds of his region.

Even with weekly day-long or half-day visits to an area, it is almost impossible to count birds over more than one or two square miles of woods and fields or accurately to cover map a larger area. In many regions of the United States large-scale maps of the countryside are available. The United States geological survey publishes contour maps that show the elevations, swampy areas, roadways, streams, and other important topographical characteristics. They will send on request an index to the topographic maps of each state. They also furnish a circular which describes how the map was made and the map symbols. The address is Map Information Office, United States Geological Survey, Department of Interior, Washington, D.C. 20241. The price per map quadrangle is $1.00. They may also be able to tell you where such maps can be obtained locally. Your state highway department is often another good source of detailed maps.

If you decide to do a population count of birds, then study my cover map of Lake Wedington carefully. Within the two square miles of the Lake Wedington area approximately 780 acres of the hills are covered with deciduous trees, mostly oak species; 148 acres are in open lands; 93 acres along streams are in mixed hardwoods; 34 acres are in brushy areas; 18 acres are in pines; 16 acres are in grasslands; and approximately 6 acres are lake-edge marshy area. These figures were arrived at by marking off the acres with a square grid on a scale map of the total area of 1,280 square acres.

The easiest method for plotting such a cover map is to pace off each of the different habitats by foot. Since the average pace is about one yard long, all of the proportions will be approximate. Some of the smaller plant areas can be spot checked by pacing to see if they each correspond in acreage to the acreage indicated by counting the squares on the grid over the topographical map (Figure 11–1). It is quite possible by pacing and checking back on the map to lay out a fairly accurate map of the different types of vegetation and habitat. Once the map is sketched out in pencil, it can be inked in with bars, dots, or other symbols to indicate the various kinds of cover. Sometimes it is possible to check your cover map from aerial photographs of the area. Such maps are most often obtained from the United States soil conservation department in your state.

In order to become familiar with the plants upon which birds feed, consult *American Wildlife and Plants, a Guide to Wildlife Food Habits* by A. C. Martin, H. S. Zim, and A. L. Nelson (New York: Dover Publications). This book gives not only the food plants of birds, but also descriptions and range maps of the favored plants of birds.

In bird census work it is very difficult to count individuals by units of area, except perhaps during the breeding season when birds more or less stay put in their nesting territory. It is relatively easy, however, to use units of time to estimate the numbers present in any one habitat. For instance, the observer might use the following time units for a habitat such as shown on the Wedington cover map: one hour censusing in the mixed hardwoods and brushy area, one-half hour in mixed oak, one-half hour in herbs and grasses, one-half hour in pine plantations, and perhaps an hour observing the lake-edge marshy areas and counting water fowl on the lake. In one four-hour morning or evening period a fairly accurate census can be taken by an observant researcher.

Such bird counts should be taken, whenever possible, during the early morning or late afternoon hours. Birds are much more conspicuous and also sing more frequently at these times, which are their main activity and feeding periods. During the summer in the heat of midday birds tend to be sedentary.

In taking bird counts it is necessary to make a judgment as to exactly how much time to spend in each habitat. The fact that more time is spent in a hardwood and brushy habitat than a pine tree habitat might raise questions as to the validity of the count for two such different areas. The reason for spending less time in a pine plantation is simply that it is usually a more open area to census. There is little brush or undergrowth, so that birds appearing in such habitats are easily spotted. Concealment is difficult where movement is easily discernible. In the Wedington study the areas of pine plantings were small and quickly covered.

As pointed out in Chapter 6 (see tables) the frequency of occurrence for each species is found by calculating the percentage of times that each species is observed out of the total number of census trips to each habitat. Thus, if the census is made during each of forty-eight weeks throughout the year, and the Carolina chickadee is observed in the flood plain areas forty-two times during those forty-eight one-hour weekly visits to that habitat, then the frequency of occurrence would be:

$^{42}/_{48}$ x 100 = 87.5 percent frequency of occurrence for the Carolina chickadee.

Another interesting relationship that can be determined from such habitat counts is called a "coefficient of community." A coefficient of community is derived by dividing the number of species common to two different habitats by the total species found in both habitats (Table 6–2). Two habitats having identical bird life would result in a coefficient of one.

For instance, if thirty of the same species were found in both the mixed oak and mixed hardwood habitats and the mixed oak and hardwood together had a total of seventy different species, then the coefficient of community between the two habitats would be: $^{30}/_{70}$ = .42. If each habitat had exactly the same species, which would not likely happen in nature, then the coefficient would be: $^{70}/_{70}$ = 1.

A table such as Table 6–2 for the Wedington habitats can be made by calculating the coefficient of community between all the various habitats. You will note that the highest coefficient of community for my study was .36 between the mixed oak and the mixed hardwood areas. If you study my cover map, you will notice one more fact about birds of these two habitats. The mixed hardwood areas (horizontal lines) that follow the stream are not usually on the edge with mixed oak, but are separated from them by herbs and grasses, a pine plantation, a road or a lake. The fact that the species of birds common to both areas are seldom seen in the intervening habitats indicates that they pass over the other habitats and do not stop to feed.

Many forest birds are insectivorous, but this does not completely explain such habitat preference. Most birds obtain their food from the most accessible sources as long as it is the type they require, thus the physical makeup of the plant type is very important. Mixed oak and mixed hardwoods are physi-

Figure 11–2. The Australian cockatoo makes an interesting pet. This one is scratching its head. Note how it brings the leg up over the wing to reach the head. Direct observation is the best way to study bird behavior.

cally very similar environments. As might be expected, the lowest similarity of species occurred between herbs and grasses and mixed oaks (a coefficient of community of .21). This may be explained on the basis that sparrows, which occur in herb and grass areas, are mostly seed eaters, and their type of food is most abundant in open areas.

Since the brush areas are included along with the mixed hardwoods as a part of the flood plain community, it is natural that there is a higher percentage of field birds in mixed hardwood than mixed oak areas (coefficient of community of .32). Brushy areas attract many seed eaters.

Pine plantations, surrounded as they are by mixed oak,

seem to be utilized by certain species from the mixed oak habitat. Woodpeckers, for example, pass freely from mixed oak to pine plantations.

It should be noted from this study, which we are using as an example, that there are only small coefficients of community between any two habitats. This indicates definite habitat selection by the various species. Data from such a study can tell us much about the ecological factors that affect the total population of different species.

ACTIVITY RECORDINGS

As Konrad Lorenz points out in his marvelous book *King Solomon's Ring*, the longing to keep pets probably arises from our desire for a bond with nature. This, of course, could be said for bird watching or even planting a flower garden. People who dwell in the suburbs or city are especially in need of such a bond.

Since this project requires the keeping of a pet bird, I would recommend that before attempting such a study my reader obtain a copy of Dr. Lorenz's book. A few leisure hours reading his humorous anecdotes about birds and animals is worth a whole course in animal behavior.

If you are lucky enough to own a pet canary, cockatoo, finch, or other such bird, then you already have a good start on the activity study (Figure 11–2). If you do not have a caged pet, then the first part of the project is to obtain a bird or birds and construct a cage for them.

The Cage

Since the cage is your pet bird's home it is important that it be of a size suitable to the bird species and easily accessible to the inside for cleaning. It is much more fun, and cheaper, to design and build your own cage than to waste money buying a fancy, ready-made cage. Although a suitable cage can be built from a wooden frame covered with wire, that type is not as sturdy or as easy to clean out as an all-wire cage. A simple way to build a strong wire cage of almost any size is illustrated in Figure 11–3.

Purchase a short segment of two-inch by four-inch mesh

Figure 11–3. A pet magpie in the author's den. A magpie makes a much better indoor pet than its large relative, the crow. The cage is three feet long by one-and-one-half feet wide and two feet high. The author describes how to build a similar cage out of this type of fence wire. This cage does not need a floor as it is placed over paper spread on a table top or floor. The magpie (Maggie) comes out the open door to play in the den while the author is writing.

heavy-duty fence wire. This type of fence wire is galvanized so it will not rust and is of a heavy enough diameter to support itself. For a two- by two-foot square cage measure out an eight-foot length of the fence wire, and cut it so that it is two and one-half feet high. A two- by two- by two and one-half-foot high cage is a good size for starlings or smaller birds such as Australian finches.

The tools that are needed to build this type of cage are heavy-duty wire cutters and a pair of pliers. Bend the eight-foot length of fence wire into a square two feet wide on each side. Leave an inch or so of cut wire sticking out at one end of the eight-foot length so that one end of the wire can be wrapped around the opposite end where the two ends are joined. Wire ends must also be left sticking up at the top of the two and one-half-foot high square of wire. A top piece two by two feet is cut out and attached by wrapping the cut ends along the top around the square top piece. To finish the bottom of the cage bend about four inches of the bottom of three sides inwards so that a two-foot square of fiberboard can slide over the turned-in wire. In order to slide the fiberboard bottom in, you will have to cut a small piece off the bottom of the fourth side. Put a perch of the proper size (or two perches) across the cage. Cut a six-inch door in one side half-way up; it can be hinged to the cage with rings of wire.

What you now have is a sturdy two-foot-square cage suitable for a medium-sized bird. The entire cage is metal and has a floor that is easily removed for cleaning or changing paper. If you obtain a bird that is able to squeeze through the two by four spacings of fence wire, then cover the whole cage with one-inch chicken wire mesh. This will keep even a small finch inside. Bird cages of any size from one-foot square up to five-feet square (magpie size) can be constructed by this method.

If you don't have a pet bird, then you may wish to get one

from the nest. If so then you are limited as to species. In the
United States almost all birds are protected by the Migratory
Bird Treaty Act. A few, such as the crow which makes a good
outdoor pet (not a caged one), are not protected. If you live
out West, you may be able to get a magpie, which makes an
excellent pet in or out of a cage (Figure 11–4). Their nests
are easy to spot along wooded waterways. Magpies, which are
almost entirely insectivorous, are still being slaughtered by
ranchers. This is unfortunate, for they are beneficial and
should be protected. Another bird which is unprotected but
ideal for a caged pet is the much-maligned starling. Not only is
it a beneficial bird, but close up it sparkles with iridescent
colors, and it is able to imitate many sounds, sometimes even
speech. It is one of the most interesting of all wild birds as a
pet.

The Starling

Starlings nest in almost any type of cavity but prefer natural cavities in trees or woodpecker holes. Entrance holes
must be larger than one and one-half inches in diameter for a
starling to pass through. Nesting holes are usually between
ten to twenty-five feet above the ground. Another good place
to look for nests is under the eaves of old barns, outbuildings,
or even houses. I have found many nests under the wood sup-
ports behind roadside billboards.

The nests are rather messy piles of loose materials such as
grass, straw, small rootlets, corn husks, or even bits of trash.
Eggs are pale bluish or greenish white to pure white. Clutch
size varies from four to six eggs.

Dr. Lorenz states in his book that the starlings develop from
hatching to first flight in about twenty-four days. He suggests
taking them from the nest at about two weeks of age. Older
birds are not tamable. Birds taken from the nest just as the

pin feathers are pushing through (eight to twelve days old) will accept a human as a foster parent. Behaviorists say that such birds are imprinted in their young minds with the form of the substitute parent so that the human is accepted as a natural bird parent. A two-week-old fledgling starling must have food shoved down his gaping mouth six or seven times a day for two weeks or so. Since starlings are mostly insectivorous, they can be raised on raw meat, such as chopped beef, bread soaked in milk, and chopped eggs. The best food, however, is insects. By consulting the author's book, *Insect Be-*

Figure 11–4.   If you live out West young magpies make excellent pets. They should be taken from the nest at about eight to ten days of age or just as the pin feathers are starting to emerge from the shafts. When they are taken young, they are "imprinted" with the image of the owner. The owner then becomes a substitute parent and the bird is much easier to tame.

havior, you can learn to build a blacklight trap that will keep you supplied with enough bugs to fill a regiment of starlings. Blacklight (long-wave ultraviolet) is highly attractive to night-flying insects. A blacklight trap is easy to build and will solve all bird-feeding problems. Remember, however, that fledgling birds must be fed at least six or seven times a day.

While the bird is a fledgling it should be kept in an artificial nesting cavity. A small, closed cardboard box with a three-inch hole in the side and rags in the bottom makes a good nesting box. Dr. Lorenz suggests that forceps be used to feed the fledgling through the hole. Since droppings are encased in a membrane they can be easily removed by the forceps. The nesting material is easy to keep clean.

The Activity Cage

Once your starling, or two if you desire, is full-grown, start to observe its behavior carefully. Notice that at certain times of day it seems to be more active or restless than at other times. Keep careful records as fall approaches, and see if it develops an activity pattern (increase of activity as the season progresses).

Although the starling in England is not considered truly migratory, most observers believe that the American-introduced starling is learning migratory habits from the large flocks of blackbirds that it associates with in spring and fall. There seems to be a certain amount of movement from the Northeast to the Southwest in the fall. It is quite possible that your starling may exhibit *Zugunruhe* (migratory restlessness).

It would be very difficult to observe your bird day in and day out, but it is possible to monitor activity continuously with a photoelectric cell unit. Such units are very inexpensive and can be bought at any good electronic store or built. (See the projects given in *Insect Behavior*.) Shine a light beam across

the cell onto the photosensitive element and connect the output
of the photocell relay to an event recorder. You may be able
to borrow such a recorder from your high school physics or
biology lab. If not, it is easy to construct one (see the projects
given in *Insect Behavior*). The light source should have a red
or green filter over it so that the bright light will not bother
your bird.

The light is directed across the cage between two perches
so that the bird will pass through the beam as it flys from
perch to perch. The recorder will show the time of day of
maxium activity. You may find out that your pet bird does
exhibit *Zugunruhe*. If it does, you may wish to vary the day
length and study the effect of light on the migratory restlessness of your bird. This can be accomplished by leaving a light
on over the cage for longer periods in the evening.

There are many ways to study behavior, but where birds
are concerned, direct observation, wherever possible, is still
one of the best. I have emphasized direct observation in these
projects because birds are beautiful creatures to observe. Bird
watching takes the researcher out into the field. These types of
projects are both enjoyable from an aesthetic sense and prac-
tical as research.

Go to work, have fun—and good luck.

Glossary

ANISODACTYL: The most common arrangement of digits (toes) in birds: the first toe (big toe or *hallux*) points backward, and the other three toes point forward.

ANTHROPOMORPHISM: The interpretation of what is not human or personal in terms of human characteristics.

APTERIUM (PL. APTERIA): The areas of bare skin between the feather tracts; on some birds they contain down.

AUDIOSPECTROGRAPH: A graph produced by special audio recording equipment that shows all of the sound frequencies, rhythms, and loudness of bird song.

AURICULAR (FEATHERS): The patch of feathers on the side of the head that covers the ear.

BARBICELS: Hair-like processes that extend as a fringe from the barbules of a feather and help hold the barbules together.

BARBS: The branches that extend from the main shaft (rachis) of a feather: the barbs from the web or vane of the feather.

BARBULES: Small filament-like branches that extend laterally from the barbs on the feather; they help hold the barbs together to form the vane.

BRISTLES: Specialized feathers that look like hair and are found around the mouth, nostrils, or eyes (eyelashes) of the bird.

BRONCHIAL TUBES: Two tubes (bronchi) that divide from the single trachea (windpipe) and go to the lungs.

CALAMUS: The hard, smooth, hollow base of the main shaft (rachis) of a feather.

CARPAL BONES: The wrist bones that lie between the fore-arm and the hand bones. There are eight carpal bones in the human hand but only two in the adult bird wing.

CARPOMETACARPUS: The bones that have fused to form the bird's hand (end of wing). The hand bones are called carpometacarpal bones in birds and are modified for flight. Most of the carpal bones of birds have fused with three metacarpal bones to form the bony support at the tip of the wing.

CERE: A soft, raised area at the base of the upper mandible in hawks, owls, and parrots. The nostrils are on the cere.

CLOACA: The common chamber into which the ducts of the digestive, excretory, and reproductive systems open. Copulating birds press the edges of their cloacae together during the transfer of sperm.

CONTOUR (FEATHERS):   The covering feathers that form the outline or contour of the bird's body.

COPULATION: The joining of the male and female for transference of sperm from the male cloaca to the female cloaca.

DIGIT: The finger bones: in birds there are only three digit bones instead of five.

DISPERSAL: Nondirectional spread of birds from their nesting site or an extension of the home range of a species.

DISPLACEMENT ACTIVITY: A form of substitution activity that occurs when the sex drive of a bird or other animal is thwarted by a partner that does not respond to a releaser signal that has been given.

DISPLAY (APPEASEMENT): A display signal that surpresses aggressiveness or escape by courting birds.

DISPLAY (EPIGAMIC): Any type of bird display that brings the male and female together and leads to copulation.

DISPLAY (POSTNUPTIAL): Any type of display between nesting pairs.

DISPLAY (THREAT): Any type of display that involves the defense of home territory.

DOWN: Soft, small feathers that lack a vein. Down is usually concealed by the contour feathers, except in the very young of certain birds, such as downy ducks.

EVOLUTION: The process of continuous change from a lower, more simple organism to a higher, more complex one. It usually takes place over a very long period of time.

FEMUR: The leg bone (thigh bone) between the body and the lower portion of the leg. In birds the thigh is hidden by feathers and skin.

FILOPLUME: Specialized feathers that are hair-like and grow in groups around the base of contour feathers.

FLEDGLING: A young bird that has just left the nest.

GONADS: The primary sex organs—ovary and testis.

GULAR POUCH: The large membranous pouch below the lower beak (mandible) of a pelican.

HABITAT: The place where a plant or animal species naturally lives and grows.

HAMULI: Hooked tips at the end of the barbicels that help hold the barbules of the feathers together.

HYOID APPARATUS: Specially modified supporting bones on the tongue. In some woodpeckers these bones curve upward and over the skull and are very long so the tongue can be protruded beyond the tip of the beak for reaching into crevices.

INFRARED LIGHT: That portion of the electromagnetic spectrum that is between visible radiation and microwave radiation; infrared waves are slightly longer than visible red (0.75 micrometers) but shorter than microwave (1,000 micrometers).

IMPRINTING: The theory of K. Z. Lorenz that young birds, during a very brief period immediately after hatching, obtain (are imprinted with) certain behavioral characteristics by observing the parents (or a substitute parent). This type of learning is considered irreversible in that the bird never forgets it.

INSECTIVOROUS: Depending on insects for food.

LARYNX: The voice box of humans and other mammals. The larynx is located at the entrance of the trachea (windpipe).

MIGRATION: The periodic directional movement of birds from one region to another.

MONOGAMY: The condition of having a single mate at any one time.

MOR: Forest humus that consists of a layer of largely organic matter distinct from the soil beneath.

MOLT (ANNUAL):   The yearly shedding or casting off of hair or feathers.

MOLT (POSTNUPTIAL):   The shedding or casting off of feathers following the nesting season.

NICHE (ECOLOGICAL):   The sum of an organism's physical and biological life-controlling factors; also, a site or habitat supplying the factors which are necessary for the successful existence of an organism.

OVARY: The female reproductive organ (usually paired) that produces the egg. Most species have only a single functional left ovary. The right ovary is undeveloped.

OVUM (PL. OVA):   A mature egg that is ready for fertilization.

OVULATION: The production of ovules (eggs in the early stage of growth) and the discharge of them from the ovary.

PAIR-BOND: The bond that is formed between the male and female and keeps them together during the nesting cycle.

PAIR FORMATION: The establishment of the pair-bond over a period of time. The time required to form the pair-bond may range from a few hours for some song birds to several months for ducks.

PECK ORDER: The arrangement of birds in a social hierarchy. Each bird is dominant to all the birds in the group below it, but subordinate to all birds above it.

PHENOLOGY: The branch of science that deals with the relationship between climate and periodic biological phenomena (events), such as the flowering of plants, fruiting of trees, migration of birds.

PHOTOPERIOD: Alternating periods of lightness and darkness that effect the growth and maturity of a living organism.

PRIMARIES: The outer feathers of a bird's wing that attach to the carpometacarpus and digital bones.

PROVENTRICULUS: The first division of the bird stomach; the proventriculus secretes the digestive enzymes.

PYGOSTYLE: The last bone of the bird's backbone (vertebrate) to which the tail feathers attach.

RACHIS: The upper part of the shaft of a feather to which vanes attach.

RADIUS: One of the bones of the forelimb between the elbow and wrist. The radius is on the thumb side of a human arm and is along the leading edge of a bird's wing.

RAPTORIAL: A bird adapted to seize prey.

RECTRICES (SING. RECTRIX):   The tail feathers of a bird.

RELEASER: Any stimulus (display signal or song) that serves to initate reflex behavior in another organism.

SECONDARIES: The inside feathers of the wing that attach to the dorsal surface of the ulna.

SEMIPLUMES: Body feathers that lack hamuli (hooklets) at the tip of the barbicels and are loose webbed and fluffy in texture.

STOOP: The swift descent of a bird of prey on the prey from a height.

SYRINX: The bird's voice box located at the end of the windpipe (trachea) where the windpipe divides to form the two bronchi.

TARSOMETATARSUS: In birds the fused tarsal and metatarsal bones. In humans the tarsal and metatarsal bones form the foot; in birds they are fused to form the long portion of the leg just above the toes (claws).

TAXONOMIST: One who studies the classification and evolution of living organisms.

TESTIS: The male reproductive gland that produces the spermatozoa; it corresponds to the ovary of the female.

TIBIA: The lower leg bone in humans; it is fused with the tarsal bone in birds to form the tibiotarsal bone.

TIBIOTARSUS: In birds the fused tibial and tarsal bones that form the upper leg (visible feathered portion). In humans the tibia is the lower portion of the leg and the tarsus is the ankle and foot bones.

TRACTS (FEATHER):   Restricted areas of the skin from which a bird's feathers grow.

TRIDACTYL: A type of foot in which the bird has only three toes instead of four. The large emus of Australia are an example.

TYMPANIC MEMBRANE: A thin membrane closing externally the cavity of the middle ear (eardrum). In birds and reptiles it is not as deeply located in the ear as in mammals.

ULNA: The second bone of the forearm. In birds it is behind the radius, and the secondary feathers attach to it.

VANES: The inner and outer webs made up of the barbs and barbules that form the feather on either side of the shaft.

VENTRICULUS: The muscular portion of the bird stomach —the gizzard.

ZUGUNRUHE: Migratory restlessness: the restless activity that is exhibited by caged birds during the normal migration period of the species.

ZYGODACTYL: A type of bird foot in which two of the digits (toes) are turned backward and two forward. Toes one and four point backward and toes two and three are turned forward. This occurs in owls, cuckoos, parrots, and woodpeckers.

Selected Reading

Allen, Arthur A. *The Book of Bird Life*. Princeton, N.J.: D. Van Nostrand Company, Inc., 1930.

Armstrong, Edward A. *Bird Display and Behavior*. New York: Oxford University Press, 1947.

Bailey, Alfred M., and Niedrach, Robert J. *Birds of Colorado*. Denver, Colo.: Denver Museum of Natural History, 1965.

Bent, Arthur Cleveland. *Life Histories of North American Birds*. Washington, D.C.: U.S. Government Printing Office, 1919–1969.

Berger, Andrew J. *Bird Study*. New York: John Wiley and Sons, Inc., 1961.

Callahan, Philip S. *Insect Behavior*. New York: Four Winds Press, 1970.

————. *The Evolution of Insects*. New York: Holiday House, 1972.

————. *The Magnificent Birds of Prey*. New York: Holiday House, 1974.

Cameron, Angus, and Parnall, Peter. *The Nightwatchers.* New York: Four Winds Press, 1971.

Carrighar, Sally. *Wild Heritage.* Boston: Houghton Mifflin Company, 1965.

Davis, L. I. *A Field Guide to the Birds of Mexico and Central America.* Austin: University of Texas Press, 1972.

Elliott, Charles, ed. *Fading Trails.* New York: The Macmillan Company, 1942.

Forbush, E. H., and May, John B. *Natural History of the Birds of Eastern and Central North America.* Boston: Houghton Mifflin Company, 1939.

Griscom, Ludlow, and Sprunt, Alexander Jr. *The Warblers of America.* Old Greenwich, Conn.: The Devin-Adair Company, 1957.

Hickey, Joseph J. *A Guide to Bird Watching.* New York: Oxford University Press, 1943.

Kortright, Francis H. *The Ducks, Geese, and Swans of North America.* Washington, D.C.: The American Wildlife Institute, 1943.

Lorenz, Konrad Z. *King Solomon's Ring.* New York: Thomas Y. Crowell Company, 1952.

Lowery, George H. *Louisiana Birds.* Baton Rouge: Louisiana State University Press, 1955.

Olsen, Jack. *Slaughter the Animals, Poison the Earth.* New York: Simon and Schuster, 1971.

Pearson, T. Gilbert, ed. *Birds of America.* Garden City, N.Y.: Garden City Publishing Company, 1936.

Peterson, Roger T. *A Field Guide to the Birds.* Boston: Houghton Mifflin Company, 1947.

Robbins, C. S., Bruun, B., Zim, H., and Singer, A. *Birds of*

North America: A Guide to Identification. New York: Golden Press, 1966.

Stefferud, Alfred, and Nelson, Arnold L., eds. *Birds in Our Lives.* New York: Arco Publishing Company, 1970.

Storer, John H. *The Web of Life: A First Book of Ecology.* Old Greenwich, Conn.: The Devin-Adair Company, 1953.

Index

activity record, 171–72
Allen, Arthur A., 16–17, 19, 39
Altum, Bernard, 96–97
American Ornithologists Union, 152
anatomy, 30–32
  gastric tract, 41–42
  reproductive tract, 55
  syrinx, 136
  wing, 24–27
Arctic tern, 127
audiospectrograph, 140–41, 152
Audubon, John James, 119
Audubon Society, The, 17, 65, 108
auk, 31–32

Bagg, A. M., 126
bald eagle, 62–63, 71
banding, 103, 124

beak
  for climbing, 43
  for defense, 42, 44, 92
  for food gathering, 41–46, 49, 51
  formation of, 30–31
behavior
  effect of evolution on, 67
  effect of form on, 20
  effect of light on, 57, 59
  monogamy, 53
  territorial rivalry, 96–97, 101. *See also* display
Bent, Arthur Cleveland, 124, 156
binoculars, 153–55
bird
  cage, 166–69
  dance, 147–48
  families, 33–37
  names, 36
  watching, 19, 51, 64
birds of North America, 36–37

birds of prey, 108–12, 114, 119
    attack of, 42
    dispersal of, 130
    molt of, 61
    talons of, 42
bittern, least, 75, 117–19
blackbird, red-winged, 13, 18–19
blue jay, 43, 84, 92
bobolink, 128
bob white, 92
breeding, 57–59
brood patch, 69
bunting, painted, 14

cage, 166–69
call
    in courtship display, 147
    of brown-capped bush tanan-
        ger, 138
    of kookaburra, 51
    of mourning dove, 14
    of red-winged blackbird, 18
    of tufted titmouse, 92. *See
        also* song
cardinal, 69, 92
chicken, American prairie, 147
classification, 33–37
cloaca, 55
cockatoo, 150
coding, 103
coefficient of community, 164
color
    display, 145
    of fledgling, 60
    for protection, 116–17
    as warning, 99, 101
comb, 30–31
communication. *See* display;
    song

copulation, 55. *See also* repro-
    duction
courtship display, 53–54, 112–
    13, 145–48
cover map, 86–90, 166
crane, 147
crossbill, red, 44–46
crow, 43, 84, 92, 169
    New Caledonian, 51
cuckoo, 31

defense, 111–19
    beak for, 42, 44
    injury feigning, 143
    song for, 136–37
    of territory, 47
diseases, 107
dispersal, 122, 128–31
displacement activity, 150
display, 53–55, 143–50
dove, mourning, 14–15, 63
Drury, William H., 146
duck, 53

eagle, 42, 53, 69, 108, 124
    bald, 62–63, 71
    golden, 39
ecology, 16–17, 111, 130, 166
egg, 67, 69
    collecting, 64–66
    incubation, 69–71, 142–43
egret, African cattle, 130
embryo, 67
emu, 147
enemies
    birds of prey, 108–11
    ground predators, 111–13
    human, 19, 112

epigamic display, 54, 143. *See also* courtship display

evolution, 21, 67

falcon, 33, 42, 108, 124

falconry, 108, 113

families, names of, 33–37

feathers, 24–29

for flight, 131–32

molt of, 60–62

feet, 31–32

feigning injury, 143

fighting, 116

finch, Galapagos, 51

fish eater, 42, 44, 51

fledgling

defense of, 115–16

food for, 39, 41

molt of, 60

as pet, 169–71

runt, 69

flight

aerodynamics of, 131–34

for defense, 111, 142

feathers for, 24–27, 131–32

migratory, 128–29

V formation, 18

flyway, 129

food

fledgling, need for, 39, 41

gathering of, 41–46, 49, 51

supply, defense of, 107

taste, sense of, 135. *See also* fish eater; grain eater; insect eater

form (shape), 28–29

for defense, 117–19

effect of environment on, 21

for identification, 155

Frederick II, 33, 64, 121

frequency of occurrence, 88, 163–64

gastric tract, 41–42

gizzard, 42

golden eagle, 39

Goldman, Peter, 141

goose, 53, 63, 134

Canada, 18

European barnacle, 64

grain eater, 41, 43–44, 92, 165

ground predator, 111–13

grouse, 53

ruffed, 82, 86

sharp-tailed, 112–13

gull

sea, 63

swallow-tailed, 61

habitat, 18, 78–79, 86

classification by, 33

coefficient of community, 164–66

cover map of, 86–90

destruction of, 19

Harris, Michael P., 61

hawk, 42, 63, 108, 119

Cooper's, 71–72

red-shouldered, 84

red-tailed, 84

sharp-shinned, 60–62

head, 30–31

heron, 44, 124, 129–30

Herrich, Francis, 71

Hickey, Joseph, 130

Howard, Henry Elliot, 97, 155

identification, 151–55, 160
    banding for, 124
    imping for, 103
Idrisi, Abu Abdullah Moham-
    med, 120
imping, 103
incubation, 69–71, 76, 142–43
injury feigning, 113–16, 143
insect eater, 49–51, 72, 82–83,
    91–92, 164

jay, blue, 43, 84, 92
junco, 82
    Oregon, 138, 141–42
    slate-colored, 57–59

Kellogg, Peter, 152
killdeer, 71, 114–16
kingfisher, 51, 78
kite, Everglade, 48–49
kiwi, 76
kookaburra, 51

Lack, David, 99–101, 107, 124
land birds, 33
leg, 32, 66
life history, 155–58
light and darkness, 57–60, 125
Lignon, J. D., 63
Lorenz, Konrad, 53, 55, 166

magpie, 35–36, 43–44, 75, 100–
    101, 106, 113, 169
    black-billed, 46–47
    yellow-billed, 38
Marler, Peter, 41
metabolism, 38–39, 127
migration, 120–29
    effect of light on, 57, 59

effect of temperature on, 57,
    59
effect of weather on, 91
V formation, 133–34
Migratory Bird Treaty Act, 169
mimicry, 119
mockingbird, 53, 137–38
Moffat, C. B., 97, 99, 101, 107
molt, 29, 60–62
monogamy, 53
morphology, 33
Moynihan, M., 138

names of birds, 36, 84
National Audubon Society, The,
    17, 65, 108
natural selection, 111, 113
nest, 71–76
neutral birds, 33
niche, 18, 78–79
nightjar, 142–43
nonmigratory species, 122
nonraptorial birds, 33
nose, 30
    sense of smell, 135–36
nuthatch, 53

omniverous birds, 46
orders, scientific names of, 33–37
ornithology, 18
ovenbird, 71–75, 82–83
owl, 20, 31, 63, 69, 108, 136
    barred, 84
    screech, 85
    long-eared, 114–15
    snowy, 130

pair bond, 53, 63
parrot, 31, 42–43

peck order, 101

pelican, 42

pet bird, 166–72

Peterson, Roger Tory, 37

phenology, 52

photoperiodism, 57–60, 125

pupit, meadow, 90

playing dead, 113

plover, 31–32

  crested, 130

population study, 161–64

postnuptial display, 54, 143

protective coloration, 116–19

quail, 119

raptorial birds, 33

raven, 53

razorbill, 150

red-winged blackbird, 13, 18–19

releaser, 148–49

reproduction, 55, 148–50

  territorial defense for, 107

  sexual maturity, 62–63

  sexual rivalry, 96–97

robin

  American, 47, 53, 75, 101–105

  English, 98–101, 105

rooster, 31

runt, 69

sandpiper, white-rumped, 146

Saunders, Aretas A., 80

scavenger, 92

Schiefflin, Eugene, 131

sea birds, 125

sea gull, 63

seed eater, 41, 43–44, 92, 165

sex differences

  display, 145

  incubation, 69, 76

  song, 136–37

shape. *See* form

signal song, 142–43

Sleeman, W. H., 65

skylark, 113

snipe, 45

  Wilson's, 117

social birds, 101, 105–106

song, 97, 99, 136–43

  recordings of, 152

sparrow, 63, 165

  field, 141–42

  fox, 57, 59

  hedge, 50

  house, 50

  white-throated, 57, 59

spring song, 55

starling, 131, 169–71

stomach, 41–42

swallow, bank, 78–79

swan, 53

syrinx, 136

talons, 42

tananger, brown-capped bush, 138

taxonomy, 21, 33

telephoto lens, 65

temperature, 38–39, 67

tern, Arctic, 127

territorial species, 97–98

threat display, 54, 101, 143

thrush, 82

tit, great, 49–50

titmouse, tufted, 92

use of tools, 50–51

V formation, 18, 133–34
Verbeek, Nicholaas A. M., 38, 75
vireo, red-eyed, 82–83
vulture, 47, 136

warbler, 60–61, 71, 83
  blackpoll, 127–28
  Kentucky, 114
  black and white, 83–84
  magnolia, 84
  wood, 42
water birds, 33
wattle, 30–31
weather, 90–92

effect on movement, 122–25,
  130
effect on nest building, 75
effect on reproduction, 57–59
weaver, 76
Weise, C. M., 57, 59
Wilson, Alexander, 84
wing, 24–27
woodpecker, 21, 31–32, 84, 90
  ivory-billed, 19
  red-cockaded, 63, 69–71, 75
  snipe, 45
wren, 39, 41

Young, Howard, 101, 107

zugunruhe, 59, 171–72